# The African Continental Free Trade Area

# The African Continental Free Trade Area
## Economic and Distributional Effects

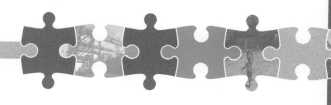

# Contents

## Tables

# Foreword

The African Continental Free Trade Area (AfCFTA) provides a unique opportunity for countries in the region to competitively integrate into the global economy, reduce poverty, and promote inclusion. Although Africa has made substantial progress in recent decades in raising living standards and reducing poverty, increasing trade can provide the impetus for reforms that boost productivity and job creation, and thereby further reduce poverty.

AfCFTA can provide this spark. By 2035, we estimate that implementing the agreement would contribute to lifting an additional 30 million people from extreme poverty and 68 million people from moderate poverty. Real income gains from full implementation of the agreement could increase by 7 percent, or nearly US$450 billion. As African economies struggle to manage the consequences of COVID-19, AfCFTA can provide an anchor for long-term reform and integration.

AfCFTA would significantly boost African trade, particularly intraregional trade in manufacturing. By 2035, the volume of total exports would increase by almost 29 percent relative to business as usual. Intracontinental exports would increase by more than 81 percent, while exports to non-African countries would rise by 19 percent. This would create new opportunities for African manufacturers and workers.

These gains would come, in part, from decreased tariffs, which remain stubbornly high in many countries in the region. Even greater gains would come from lowering trade costs by reducing nontariff barriers and improving hard and soft infrastructure at the borders—so-called trade facilitation measures. These measures would reduce red tape, lower compliance costs for traders, and ultimately make it easier for African businesses to integrate into global supply chains. These reforms would be difficult, but the rewards would be substantial.

Freer intra-African trade would help women by lowering the gender wage gap, and it would help all workers by increasing decent employment opportunities. A growing manufacturing sector would provide new job opportunities, especially for women. The report estimates that compared with a business-as-usual scenario, implementing AfCFTA would lead to an almost 10 percent increase in wages, with larger gains for unskilled workers and women.

This report is designed to guide policy makers as they continue the process of negotiating and implementing the agreement. Creating a continent-wide market will require a determined effort to reduce all trade costs. This will require legislation to enable goods, capital, and information to flow freely and easily across the African borders. Competitive business environments will boost productivity and investment. Increased foreign competition will put pressure on domestic firms to increase productivity or risk losing market share. For most African firms, the best way to raise productivity and increase market share will be to invest in technological capabilities that enable them to develop domestic and regional value chains while taking advantage of the opportunities offered by global value chains.

In the few sectors where AfCFTA's implementation results in job losses, governments will need to be ready to support workers with adequate safety nets and policies to retrain them. Policy makers will also have to prepare for AfCFTA's distributional impacts—across sectors and countries, on skilled and unskilled workers, and on female and male workers. Doing so will enable them to design policies to increase the readiness of their workforce to take advantage of new opportunities.

AfCFTA is a major opportunity for Africa, but implementation will be a significant challenge. Lowering tariffs is only the first step. Reforming nontariff and trade facilitation measures will require substantial policy reforms at the national level. These reforms may require politically difficult decisions in some cases. However, the agreement's opportunities can be used to help policy makers overcome these challenges and implement the substantive reforms that are needed to make Africa as competitive as any other region in the world.

**Caroline Freund**
Global Director, Trade, Competition and Investment,
World Bank

**Albert Zeufack**
Chief Economist, Africa Region,
World Bank

# Acknowledgments

This study was written by Maryla Maliszewska (Senior Economist, Trade and Regional Integration Unit [ETIRI]) and Michele Ruta (Lead Economist, ETIRI), with Guillermo Carlos Arenas (Economist, ETIRI), Paul Brenton (Lead Economist, ETIRI), Cesar Calderon (Lead Economist, AFECE), Roberto Echandi (Lead Economist, ETIRI), Erik Churchill (Consultant, ETIRI), Claudia Hofmann (Consultant, ETIRI), Israel Osorio-Rodarte (Economist, ETIRI), Maria Filipa Seara e Pereira (Consultant, ETIRI), Yulia Vnukova (Consultant, ETIRI), and Dominique Van Der Mensbrugghe (Research Professor and Director, Global Trade Analysis Project [GTAP] Center at Purdue University).

This report is an output of Trade and Regional Integration Unit in close collaboration with the Africa Chief Economist Office of the World Bank and African Union Commission. The Commissioner for Trade and Industry, Mr. Albert Muchanga; Africa Region Chief Economist Mr. Albert Zeufack; Global Director Ms. Caroline Freund; and ETIRI Practice Manager, Mr. Antonio Nucifora provided guidance and supervision.

Joseph Rebello provided guidance on communications strategy. All finalized papers, data, and blogs have been posted on the World Bank website created and maintained by Erin Scronce and Torie Smith and are available at https://www.worldbank.org/en/topic/trade/publication/african-continental-free-trade-agreement.

The study also benefited from the comments of Erhan Artuc (Senior Economist, DECTI), Kathleen Beegle (Lead Economist, HGNDR), Michael Ferrantino (Lead Economist, GMTRI), Stephen Karingi (UNECA), Deeksha Kokas (Consultant, EPVGE), Csilla Lakatos (Senior Economist, EPGDR), Gladys Lopez Acevedo (Lead Economist, EMNPV), Simon Mevel-Bidaux (UNECA), Ambar Narayan (Lead Economist, EPVGE), Vijay Pillai (Adviser, AFRVP), and Bob Rijkers (Senior Economist, DECTI).

We are grateful for the valuable insights and collaboration of several colleagues from the African Union Commission: Prudence Sebahizi (Chief Technical Advisor and Head of AfCFTA Unit), Million Habte Begna (Senior Expert on Trade in Services), Oswald Chinyamakobvu (Expert on Technical Barriers to Trade), Beatrice Claudia Chaytor (Senior Expert on Trade in Services), Halima Noor Abdi (Senior Expert on Trade in Goods), Roslyn Ng'eno (Expert on Investment), Youssouf Hamid Takane (Program Manager), and Willie Shumba (Senior Expert on Customs).

Many colleagues, inside and outside the World Bank Group, provided useful suggestions and inputs at various stages: Alvaro Espitia Rueda, Michael J. Ferrantino, Woubet Kassa, Maria Liungman, Nadia P. Rocha Gaffurri, Karen Souza Muramatsu, Jose E. Signoret, Javiera C. Petersen Muga, Huanjun Zhang, Cristian Ignacio Jara Nercasseau, Raimundo Smith Mayer, and Claudio E. Montenegro.

Guillermo Varela and Estudio Prado created the concept for the cover illustration. Kirsten Dennison developed the cover and interior design. Sabra Ledent edited the text. Patricia Katayama and Mary Fisk managed the publishing process. Orlando Mota was the print and electronic conversion coordinator.

The team also thanks Cynthia Abidin-Saurman, Tanya Cubbins, and Flavia Nahmias da Silva Gomes in Washington, D.C., for their assistance in preparing this report and for their support of the project.

# About the Authors

**Maryla Maliszewska**, the lead author, is a Senior Economist in the Trade and Regional Integration Unit (ETIRI) at the World Bank. Her area of expertise covers various aspects of trade policy and regional integration, with a special focus on the impacts of trade on poverty and income distribution. Her research also covers global analyses of structural change, demographic transition, and pandemics, using computable general equilibrium models. She has published in journals such as the *Review of Development Economics*, the *Journal of Policy Modeling*, the *Journal of African Economies*, and several World Bank flagships. She was a Research Fellow at the Center for Social and Economic Research in Warsaw, Poland. She holds a PhD from the University of Sussex in Brighton, UK, and an MA in economics from Sussex and Warsaw University.

**Michele Ruta** is a Lead Economist in ETIRI. His research interests are in international economics, particularly issues concerning international and regional integration. He has published in refereed journals, such as the *Journal of International Economics*, the *Journal of Public Economics*, and the *Journal of the European Economic Association*. He was a lead author of the *World Trade Report* of the World Trade Organization (WTO) from 2008 to 2013. He had previous appointments as Economic Adviser at the World Bank, Senior Economist at the International Monetary Fund, Counsellor at the WTO, and Marie Curie Fellow at the European University Institute. He holds a PhD in economics from Columbia University and an undergraduate degree from the University of Rome "La Sapienza."

# About the Contributors

**Guillermo Arenas** is an Economist in the Trade and Regional Integration Unit (ETIRI) at the World Bank. His area of expertise covers various aspects of international economics and public policy, including trade policy, export competitiveness, and impact evaluation. He specializes in the microeconomic analysis of trade and fiscal policies using firm-level data. He holds a master's of public administration degree from Syracuse University.

**Paul Brenton** is a Lead Economist in ETIRI. He focuses on analytical and operational work on trade and regional integration. He recently coauthored the joint World Bank–World Trade Organization report, *The Role of Trade in Ending Poverty*. He has managed a range of policy-oriented volumes, including *De-Fragmenting Africa: Deepening Regional Trade Integration in Goods and Services, Africa Can Help Feed Africa,* and *Carbon Footprints and Food Systems: Do Current Accounting Methodologies Disadvantage Developing Countries?* Prior to joining the World Bank in 2002, he was a Senior Research Fellow and head of the Trade Policy Unit at the Centre for European Policy Studies in Brussels. He has a PhD in economics from the University of East Anglia. A collection of his work has been published in *International Trade, Distribution and Development: Empirical Studies of Trade Policies.*

**César Calderón** is a Lead Economist in the Chief Economist Office of the Africa Region at the World Bank. Before joining the Bank, he was a Senior Economist in the Research Department of the Central Bank of Chile. He has worked on issues of growth and development, especially the growth effects of infrastructure development and outward-oriented strategies. He has also worked on issues of capital flows and their link to financial imbalances. He is currently working on drivers of capital flows, macroeconomic vulnerabilities, and the microeconomics of aggregate productivity in Sub-Saharan Africa. He holds an MA and a PhD in economics from the University of Rochester.

**Roberto Echandi** is a Lead Private Sector Specialist in ETIRI. His current work program focuses on research and policy advice on issues related to cross-border trade in services, negotiation, implementation and maximization of potential benefits of deep integration trade agreements, and the AfCFTA negotiation and implementation process. Prior to joining the World Bank trade unit, he was the Global Lead for Investment Policy and Promotion of the Trade and Competitiveness Global Practice. Previously, he was Director of the Program on International Investment at the World Trade Institute (WTI) of the University of Bern. He is also a member of the faculty of the masters in international law and economics at the WTI and a member of the editorial board of the *Journal of World Investment and Trade*. He has also recently been a member of the faculty of the masters in international economic law at the University of Barcelona and a member of the editorial board of the *Journal of International Economic Law*.

**Dominique van der Mensbrugghe** is Research Professor and Director of the Center for Global Trade Analysis at Purdue University. Prior to joining Purdue, he worked at a trio of international agencies—as Senior Economist and Team Leader at the Food and Agriculture Organization, Lead Economist at the World Bank, and Senior Economist at the Organisation for Economic Co-operation and Development. The focus of his work during his career has been on long-term structural change of the global economy and the analysis of global economic policy issues. His work has appeared frequently in various economic journals and agencies' flagship reports, and he is one of the world's experts on global computable general equilibrium modeling. He received his undergraduate degree in mathematics at the Université Catholique de Louvain in Belgium and a PhD in economics from the University of California, Berkeley.

**Israel Osorio Rodarte** is an Economist in ETIRI. He has more than 10 years of experience in international development, particularly in the areas of economic diversification, structural change, and distributional analysis of trade and macroeconomic policy. Before joining the World Bank, he consulted for think tanks and international organizations, such as the German Development Institute, the Organisation for Economic Co-operation and Development, the United Nations, and the Inter-American Development Bank. His academic research has been published in the *Review of Development Economics*, the *Journal of Policy Modeling*, and the *Journal of African Economies and World Development*, as well as several World Bank flagships. He holds an MA in economics and public policy from Georgetown University and Tecnológico de Monterrey.

**Maria Filipa Seara e Pereira** is a consultant in ETIRI. She works mainly on topics of international trade and international development, particularly in modeling, trade policy, and the distributional effects of trade and global value chains. She has participated in several World Bank publications, including *Trading for Development in the Age of Global Value Chains* and "Western Balkans Regular Economic Report." Before joining the World Bank, she worked for the Embassy of Portugal in the United States as an economic affairs research assistant following the Trans-Atlantic Trade and Investment Partnership agreement and several anti-dumping cases. She holds a master's degree in international policy and practice, with economics and international trade specialization, from the George Washington University and a master's degree in political science from the Catholic University of Portugal.

**Yulia Vnukova** is a consultant in ETIRI. Based on more than 10 years of experience, her current work focuses on trade policy and regional integration, with the focus on macroeconomic and microeconomic analysis of trade, trade and sector competitiveness, global value chains, and private sector development in emerging economies across Africa, Asia, and Europe. Her recent research focuses on estimating the economic and fiscal impact of trade policies in partial and general equilibrium environments, such as the impact of the 2018 US-China trade war. Before joining the World Bank, she worked at the United Nations. She holds a master's degree in international economics and finance from the Johns Hopkins University School of Advanced International Studies.

# Abbreviations

| | |
|---|---|
| AfCFTA | African Continental Free Trade Area |
| AGOA | African Growth and Opportunity Act |
| AU | African Union |
| AVE | ad valorem equivalent |
| BIAT | Boosting Intra-Africa Trade |
| CDE | constant differences in elasticity |
| CEMAC | Economic and Monetary Community of Central Africa |
| CEN-SAD | Community of Sahel-Saharan States |
| CES | constant-elasticity-of-substitution |
| CET | common external tariff |
| CET | constant-elasticity-of-transformation |
| CGE | computable general equilibrium |
| CIF | cost, insurance, and freight |
| COMESA | Common Market for East and South Africa |
| CwA | Compact with Africa |
| EAC | East African Community |
| EBA | Everything But Arms |
| ECCAS | Economic Community of Central African States |
| ECOWAS | Economic Community of West African States |
| EFTA | European Free Trade Association |
| EV | equivalent variation |
| FDI | foreign direct investment |
| FOB | free on board |
| GATS | General Agreement on Trade in Services |
| GDP | gross domestic product |
| GIDD | Global Income Distribution Dynamics |
| GMD | Global Micro Database |
| GTAP | Global Trade Analysis Project |
| I2D2 | International Income Distribution Database |
| IAM | Integrated Assessment Modeling |

| | |
|---|---|
| ICT | information and communications technology |
| IGAD | Intergovernmental Authority on Development |
| IIASA | International Institute for Applied Systems Analysis |
| ILO | International Labour Organization |
| IPR | intellectual property rights |
| ISIC | International Standard Industrial Classification |
| ISO | International Organization for Standardization |
| LCU | local currency unit |
| LDC | least developed country |
| LES | linear expenditure system |
| LIS | Luxembourg Income Study |
| MFN | most favored nation |
| NEC | not elsewhere classified |
| NES | not elsewhere specified |
| NTB | nontariff barrier |
| OECD | Organisation for Economic Co-operation and Development |
| PIK | Potsdam Institute for Climate Impact Research |
| PPML | Pseudo-Poisson Maximum Likelihood |
| PTA | preferential trade agreement |
| REC | regional economic community |
| RTA | regional trade agreement |
| SACU | South African Customs Union |
| SADC | South African Development Community |
| SCM | Synthetic Control Method |
| SPS | sanitary and phytosanitary |
| SSCBT | small-scale cross-border trade |
| SSP | socioeconomic pathway |
| STE | state trading enterprise |
| TASTE | Tariff Analytical and Simulation Tool for Economists |
| TBT | technical barrier to trade |
| TF | trade facilitation |
| TFA | trade facilitation agreement |
| TRIPS | Trade-Related Aspects of Intellectual Property Rights |
| TRIST | Tariff Reform Impact Simulation Tool |
| UMA | Arab Maghreb Union |
| VAT | value added tax |
| WAEMU | West African Economic and Monetary Union |
| WITS | World Integrated Trade Solution |
| WTO | World Trade Organization |

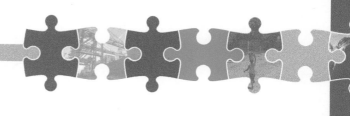

# Overview

The African Continental Free Trade Area (AfCFTA) agreement will create the largest free trade area in the world measured by the number of countries participating. The pact connects 1.3 billion people across 55 countries with a combined gross domestic product (GDP) valued at US$3.4 trillion. It has the potential to lift 30 million people out of extreme poverty, but achieving its full potential will depend on putting in place significant policy reforms and trade facilitation measures. As the global economy is in turmoil due to the COVID-19 pandemic, creation of the vast AfCFTA regional market is a major opportunity to help African countries diversify their exports, accelerate growth, and attract foreign direct investment.

The scope of AfCFTA is large. The agreement will reduce tariffs among member countries and cover policy areas such as trade facilitation and services, as well as regulatory measures such as sanitary standards and technical barriers to trade. It will complement existing subregional economic communities and trade agreements in Africa by offering a continent-wide regulatory framework and by regulating policy areas—such as investment and intellectual property rights protection (table O.1)—that so far have not been covered in most subregional agreements in Africa.

## DATA AND METHODOLOGY

This analysis quantifies the long-term economic and distributional implications of AfCFTA. It assesses the implications for economic growth, international trade, poverty, and employment, including for female and male workers. It quantifies the short- and long-term implications of tariff revenue. The analysis relies on a global computable general equilibrium (CGE) model and a microsimulation framework to quantify the agreement's impact. The CGE model is calibrated to the most recent database produced by the Global Trade Analysis Project (GTAP). The GTAP database is supplemented by additional data that quantify other barriers to trade. To date, studies on the economic implications of Africa's regional integration have mainly focused on tariff and nontariff barriers (NTBs) in goods. This analysis extends those studies to cover NTBs in services and trade facilitation measures. Most important, the analysis is extended to investigate the implications of AfCFTA for poverty, impacts on unskilled workers, and women.

Table O.1    Overview of policy areas covered in Africa's subregional PTAs and AfCFTA

| | East African Community (EAC) | Common Market for East and South Africa (COMESA) | South African Development Community (SADC) | Economic Community of West African States (ECOWAS) | West African Economic and Monetary Union (WAEMU) | South African Customs Union (SACU) | Economic and Monetary Community of Central Africa (CEMAC) | African Continental Free Trade Area (AfCFTA) |
|---|---|---|---|---|---|---|---|---|
| Tariffs on manufactured goods | ✓ | ✓ | ✓ | ✓ | ✓ | ✓ | ✓ | ✓ |
| Tariffs on agricultural goods | ✓ | ✓ | ✓ | ✓ | ✓ | ✓ | ✓ | ✓ |
| Export taxes | ✗ | ✓ | ✓ | ✗ | ✓ | ✗ | ✓ | ✓ |
| Customs | ✓ | ✓ | ✓ | ✓ | ✗ | ✓ | ✗ | ✓ |
| Competition policy | ✓ | ✓ | ✓ | ✗ | ✓ | ✓ | ✓ | ✓ |
| State aid | ✓ | ✓ | ✓ | ✓ | ✗ | ✗ | ✓ | ✗ |
| Antidumping | ✗ | ✓ | ✓ | ✗ | ✗ | ✗ | ✗ | ✓ |
| Countervailing measures | ✗ | ✓ | ✗ | ✗ | ✗ | ✗ | ✗ | ✓ |
| STEs | ✗ | ✗ | ✓ | ✗ | ✗ | ✓ | ✓ | ✓ |
| TBTs | ✓ | ✓ | ✓ | ✓ | ✓ | ✗ | ✓ | ✓ |
| GATS | ✓ | ✓ | ✓ | ✓ | ✗ | ✓ | ✓ | ✓ |
| SPS measures | ✓ | ✓ | ✓ | ✓ | ✗ | ✗ | ✓ | ✓ |
| Movement of capital | ✓ | ✓ | ✗ | ✓ | ✓ | ✗ | ✗ | ✓ |
| Public procurement | ✓ | ✗ | ✗ | ✗ | ✗ | ✗ | ✗ | ✗ |
| IPRs | ✓ | ✗ | ✓ | ✗ | ✗ | ✗ | ✗ | ✓ |
| Investment | ✓ | ✓ | ✗ | ✓ | ✗ | ✗ | ✓ | ✓ |
| Environmental laws | ✓ | ✓ | ✗ | ✗ | ✗ | ✗ | ✗ | ✗ |
| Labor market regulations | ✓ | ✓ | ✗ | ✗ | ✗ | ✗ | ✗ | ✗ |

Source: Based on Hofmann, Osnago, and Ruta (2017).

Note: ✓ = policy area covered; ✗ = policy area not covered; AfCFTA = African Continental Free Trade Area; GATS = General Agreement on Trade in Services; IPRs = intellectual property rights; PTAs = preferential trade agreements; SPS = sanitary and phytosanitary; STEs = state trading enterprises; TBTs = technical barriers to trade.

The forward-looking scenarios were designed using the global dynamic CGE model and the global microsimulation framework Global Income Distribution Dynamics (GIDD). This approach allows analysis of global development and structural transformation, incorporating the complex interactions of productivity differences at the country, sector, or factor level; shifts in demand as income rises; demographic and skill dynamics in factor markets; and changes in comparative advantage and trade flows from globalization or trade liberalization. Analysis of distributional outcomes of AfCFTA required (1) building a new data set on the employment and wages of female and male workers at the industry level across AfCFTA members; (2) building a gender-sensitive CGE model; and (3) updating several household surveys to be used in the microsimulations.

In line with ongoing negotiations, the model assumes reductions in tariff and non-tariff barriers and in trade facilitation bottlenecks. Specifically:

- Tariffs on intracontinental trade are reduced progressively in line with AfCFTA modalities. Starting in 2020, tariffs on 90 percent of tariff lines will be eliminated over a 5-year period (10 years for least developed countries, or LDCs). Starting in 2025, tariffs on an additional 7 percent of tariff lines will be eliminated over a five-year period (eight years for LDCs). Up to 3 percent of tariff lines that account for no more than 10 percent of intra-Africa imports could be excluded from liberalization by the end of 2030 (2033 for LDCs).
- Nontariff barriers on both goods and services are reduced on a most-favored-nation (MFN) basis. It is assumed that 50 percent of NTBs can be addressed with policy changes within the context of AfCFTA—with a cap of 50 percentage points. It is also assumed that additional reductions of NTBs on exports will be forthcoming.
- AfCFTA will be accompanied by measures that facilitate trade through implementation of a trade facilitation agreement (TFA). Estimates of the size of these trade barriers were provided by de Melo and Sorgho (2019). These are halved, although capped at 10 percentage points.

## MACROECONOMIC IMPACTS OF AfCFTA

Real income gains from full implementation of AfCFTA could increase by 7 percent by 2035, or nearly US$450 billion (in 2014 prices and market exchange rates). But the aggregate numbers mask the heterogeneity of impacts across countries and sectors. At the very high end are Côte d'Ivoire and Zimbabwe with income gains of 14 percent each (figure O.1). At the low end, a few countries would see real income gains of around 2 percent—including Madagascar, Malawi, and Mozambique. Real income gains from tariff liberalization alone are small, about 0.2 percent at the continental level, although some countries would record gains of more than 1 percent. Constraints to African trade are largely attributable to the high costs of that trade. As a result, the biggest

**Figure O.1**    Real income gains, by country and policy reform

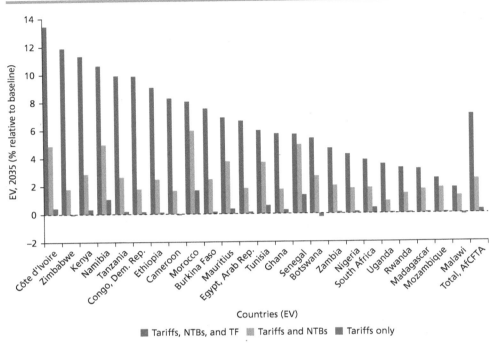

Source: Estimates, World Bank study team.

*Note:* Equivalent variation (EV) is the expenditure to attain utility in year *t* in any given simulation using base year prices. NTB = nontariff barrier; TF = trade facilitation.

gains would come from the reduction in NTBs and implementation of the TFA. Under combined tariff liberalization and reduction in NTBs, the real income gain would amount to 2.4 percent in 2035 at the continental level. The biggest boost would arise from implementation of the TFA, which would raise the gains for AfCFTA members to 7 percent of income.

AfCFTA would significantly boost African trade, particularly intraregional trade in manufacturing. The volume of total exports would increase by almost 29 percent by 2035 relative to the baseline. Intracontinental exports would increase by over 81 percent, while exports to non-African countries would rise by 19 percent. Intra-AfCFTA exports to AfCFTA partners would rise especially fast for Cameroon, the Arab Republic of Egypt, Ghana, Morocco, and Tunisia, with exports doubling or tripling with respect to the baseline. Under the AfCFTA scenario, manufacturing exports would gain the most, 62 percent overall, with intra-Africa trade increasing by 110 percent and exports to the rest of the world rising by 46 percent. Smaller gains would be observed in agriculture—49 percent for intra-Africa trade and 10 percent for extra-Africa trade. The gains in the services trade are more modest—about 4 percent overall and 14 percent within Africa.

The AfCFTA agreement would also boost regional output and productivity and lead to a reallocation of resources across sectors and countries. By 2035, total production of the continent would be almost US$212 billion higher than the baseline. Output would increase the most in natural resources and services (1.7 percent), with manufacturing seeing a 1.2 percent rise. But output in agriculture would contract 0.5 percent (relative to the baseline in 2035) at the continental level. In absolute terms, most of the gains would be realized by the services sector (US$147 billion), with smaller gains in manufacturing (US$56 billion) and natural resources (US$17 billion). By 2035, agricultural output would decline by US$8 billion relative to the baseline. As compared with the baseline in 2035, agriculture is growing faster in all parts of Africa except for North Africa, which under AfCFTA is shifting toward manufacturing and services.

The aggregate numbers, however, mask the heterogeneity of impacts across countries and sectors. Ninety percent of countries would see their volume of services grow under AfCFTA, reflecting in part the higher demand for services as Africa's economy grows. Similarly, 60 percent of countries would see growth in the value of their output of agricultural and manufacturing goods.

AfCFTA's short-term impact on tax revenues is small for most countries. Tariff revenues would decline by less than 1.5 percent for 49 out of 54 countries. Total tax revenues would decline by less than 0.3 percent in 50 out of 54 countries. Two factors help explain these small revenue impacts. First, only a small share of tariff revenues come from imports from African countries (less than 10 percent on average). Second, exclusion lists can shield most tariff revenues from liberalization because these revenues are highly concentrated in a few tariff lines (1 percent of tariff lines account for more than three-quarters of tariff revenues in almost all African countries). In the medium to long run, tariff revenues would grow by 3 percent by 2035 relative to the baseline as imports rise and as tariff liberalization is accompanied by a reduction in NTBs and implementation of trade facilitation measures.

## DISTRIBUTIONAL IMPACTS OF AfCFTA ON POVERTY AND EMPLOYMENT

AfCFTA can lift an additional 30 million people from extreme poverty (1.5 percent of the continent's population) and 68 million people from moderate poverty (figure O.2). In 2015, the latest year for which detailed World Bank estimates are available, 415 million people in Africa lived in extreme poverty (at US$1.90 a day in purchasing power parity, PPP, terms). Across the continent, however, poverty rates vary widely by region—for example, from 41.1 percent in Sub-Saharan Africa to less than 3 percent in North Africa. By country, the poverty rate is 77.7 percent in the Central African Republic, but just 0.4 percent in Algeria and Egypt. Under baseline simulations, the headcount ratio of extreme poverty in Africa is projected to decline to 10.9 percent by 2035 from 34.7 percent in the latest estimate (2015). Full implementation of AfCFTA

**Figure O.2**   Evolution of extreme and moderate poverty under baseline and AfCFTA
implementation, 2015–35

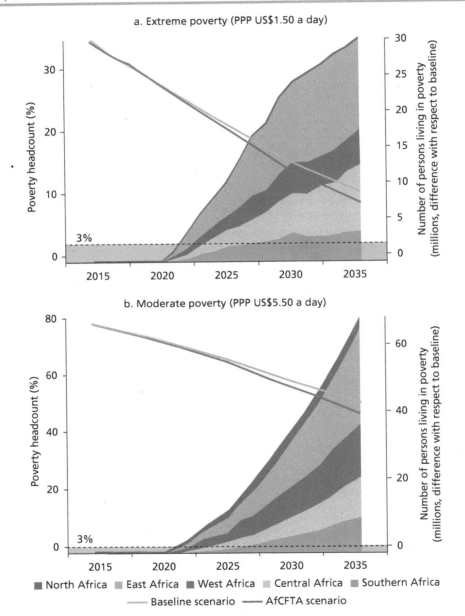

Source: Estimates, World Bank study team.

Note: The dashed line indicates the World Bank target for reducing the global poverty headcount ratio to
3 percent by 2030. For moderate poverty, the 3 percent target is only indicative. Central Africa = Angola,
Cameroon, Central African Republic, Chad, Democratic Republic of Congo, Equatorial Guinea, Gabon, Republic
of Congo, Rwanda, São Tomé and Príncipe; East Africa = Burundi, Comoros, Djibouti, Eritrea, Ethiopia, Kenya,
Somalia, South Sudan, Sudan, Uganda; North Africa = Algeria, Arab Republic of Egypt, Libya, Morocco, Tunisia;
southern Africa = Botswana, Eswatini, Lesotho, Madagascar, Malawi, Mauritius, Mozambique, Namibia,
the Seychelles, South Africa, Tanzania, Zambia, Zimbabwe; West Africa = Benin, Burkina Faso, Cabo Verde,
Côte d'Ivoire, Ghana, Guinea, Guinea-Bissau, Liberia, Mali, Mauritania, Niger, Nigeria, Senegal ,Sierra Leone,
The Gambia, Togo. AfCFTA = African Continental Free Trade Area; PPP = purchasing power parity.

would contribute to a further decline by lifting an additional 30 million from extreme poverty. In West Africa, the poverty headcount would decline by 12 million people, while the decline for Central and East Africa would be 9.3 million and 4.8 million, respectively. At the moderate poverty line of PPP US$5.50 a day, AfCFTA has the potential to lift 67.9 million people, or 3.6 percent of the continent's population, out of poverty by 2035.

Implementation of AfCFTA would increase employment opportunities and wages for unskilled workers and help to close the gender wage gap. The continent would see a net increase in the proportion of workers in energy-intensive manufacturing. Agricultural employment would increase in 60 percent of countries, and wages for unskilled labor would grow faster where there is an expansion in agricultural employment. By 2035, wages for unskilled labor would be 10.3 percent higher than the baseline; the increase for skilled workers would be 9.8 percent. Wages would grow slightly faster for women than for men as output expands in key female labor–intensive industries. By 2035, wages for women would increase 10.5 percent with respect to the baseline, compared with 9.9 percent for men.

Labor market results would vary by country, and some workers would lose jobs even as others gain new job opportunities and higher wages. Governments will need to focus on facilitating a smooth and inclusive transition by supporting flexible labor markets, improving connectivity within countries, and maintaining sound macroeconomic policies and a business environment that is friendly to domestic and foreign investors. Policy makers will need to carefully monitor AfCFTA's distributional impacts—across sectors and countries, on skilled and unskilled workers, and on female and male workers. Doing so will enable them to design policies to reduce the costs of job switching and provide effective safety nets where they are needed most.

## THE AFRICAN CONTINENTAL FREE TRADE AREA IS A KEY TO HELP AFRICA ADDRESS THE CHALLENGES OF COVID-19

The COVID-19 pandemic has taken a toll on human life and brought major disruption to economic activity across the world. Despite arriving later in Sub-Saharan Africa, the virus has spread rapidly across the continent. Economic growth in the region is projected to decline from 2.4 percent in 2019 to between −2.1 percent to −5.1 percent in 2020, the first recession in the past quarter century (World Bank 2020). It will cost the region between US$37 billion and US$79 billion in terms of output losses for 2020. The downward growth revision in 2020 reflects the macroeconomic risks arising from the sharp decline in output growth among the region's key trading partners, the fall in commodity prices, and the reduced tourism, as well as the effects of measures to contain the pandemic. The COVID-19 crisis is also contributing to increased food insecurity as currencies are weakening and prices of staple foods are rising in many parts of the region.

Policy responses that result in subregional trade blockages will increase transaction costs and lead to even larger welfare losses. In Sub-Saharan Africa, these policies will disproportionately impact household welfare as a result of price increases and supply shortages. Welfare losses would amount to 14 percent relative to the no-COVID scenario if countries were to close their borders to trade (World Bank 2020). Border closings have disproportionally affected the poor, particularly small-scale cross-border traders, agricultural workers, and unskilled workers in the informal sector. The COVID-19 pandemic has laid bare the deficiencies in trade facilitation and border management procedures, as many of these countries have struggled with efforts to keep trade moving while increasing imports of essential supplies and mitigating the spread of the disease.

In this context, a successful implementation of AfCFTA would be crucial. In the short term, the agreement would help cushion the negative effects of COVID-19 on economic growth by supporting regional trade and value chains through the reduction of trade costs. In the longer term, AfCFTA would allow countries to anchor expectations by providing a path for integration and growth-enhancing reforms. Furthermore, the pandemic has demonstrated the need for increased cooperation among trading partners. By replacing the patchwork of regional agreements, streamlining border procedures, and prioritizing trade reforms, AfCFTA could help countries increase their resiliency in the face of future economic shocks.

## CAVEATS

This analysis comes with several caveats. On the one hand, the results may underestimate the impacts of AfCFTA because they do not capture (1) informal trade flows or new trade flows in sectors and countries that are not trading in the baseline; (2) dynamic gains from trade (such as productivity increases, economies of scale, and learning by doing); and (3) foreign direct investment (FDI)—improving market conditions, competitiveness, and business sentiment will likely stimulate FDI in Africa, thereby leading to higher investment and accelerating imports of higher-technology intermediate and capital goods and improved management practices. Therefore, FDI inflows could boost regional income well above the gains predicted in this analysis. On the other hand, the results may overestimate the impacts of AfCFTA because the analysis does≈not capture (1) the costs of lowering nontariff barriers and trade facilitation measures; and (2) the transitional costs associated with trade-related structural change such as employment shifts and potentially stranded assets such as capital. Furthermore, the results are based on a new data set on gender-disaggregated employment and wages, which requires further vetting by country experts.

AfCFTA offers big opportunities for development in Africa, but implementation will be a significant challenge. This analysis identifies key priorities for African policy makers. Lowering and eliminating tariffs will be the relatively easy part—even if it comes, in some cases, with the challenge of how to replace tariff revenues. The hard part will be enacting the nontariff and trade facilitation measures, which is where the analysis predicts the largest potential economic gains. Such measures will require substantial policy reforms at the national level, indicating a long road ahead. Achieving AfCFTA's full potential depends on agreeing to ambitious liberalization and implementing it in full. Partial reforms would lead to smaller effects.

## REFERENCES

de Melo, J., and Z. Sorgho. 2019. "The Landscape of Rules of Origin across African RECs in a Comparative Perspectives with Suggestions for Harmonization." Fondation pour Les Études et Recherches sur le Développement International, Clermont-Ferrand, France.

Hofmann, Claudia, Alberto Osnago, and Michele Ruta. 2017. "Horizontal Depth: A New Database on the Content of Preferential Trade Agreements." Policy Research Working Paper 7981, World Bank, Washington, DC.

World Bank. 2020. *Africa's Pulse* 21, World Bank, Washington, DC.

# 1 Introduction

On March 21, 2018, at the 10th Extraordinary Summit of the African Union, almost all countries on the African continent signed the African Continental Free Trade Area (AfCFTA) agreement, thereby creating the largest free trade area in the world. The agreement connected 55 countries and 1.3 billion people. The combined gross domestic product (GDP) of AfCFTA economies is valued at US$3.4 trillion.

The agreement officially entered into force on May 30, 2019, after ratification of the agreement by 22 countries (figure 1.1).

AfCFTA addresses the long-standing economic fragmentation of Africa. Trade barriers remain high across the continent. Although statutory tariffs have been reduced to below 5 percent for roughly half of the countries, they remain high for sensitive sectors. Many other barriers are restricting continental economic integration as well— nontariff barriers in services and other sectors, weak and fragmented rules aimed at promoting investment and competition, and inadequate institutions such as customs management to facilitate trade.

Africa accounts for less than 3 percent of global trade and GDP, but 16.7 percent of global population (figure 1.2). The signatory countries trade little with each other—less than 8 percent of their exports are directed to other prospective member countries. Even compared with all intraregional trade in Africa (around 11 percent), this share is low, suggesting that the growth of regional trade is subject to important constraints.

Poverty reduction remains a critical priority in Africa. The poverty headcount ratio (percentage of the population living below the poverty line of US$1.90 a day) is high in AfCFTA countries, averaging 32.2 percent. Ratios range from 77.8 percent for Madagascar to 0.5 percent for Algeria and Mauritius.[1]

This study assesses the potential economic implications of AfCFTA, quantifying the impacts using a computable general equilibrium (CGE) model calibrated to the most recent database produced by the Global Trade Analysis Project (GTAP).[2] The GTAP database is supplemented by data that quantify some of the other barriers to trade that, if part of the integration package, could support the elimination of tariffs in boosting trade integration and accelerating growth. To date, macroeconomic studies on the economic implications of Africa's regional integration have mainly focused on

**Figure 1.1**    AfCFTA member countries, by status of ratification

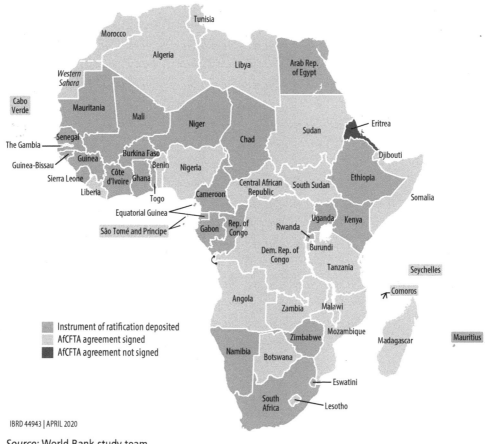

IBRD 44943 | APRIL 2020

*Source:* World Bank study team.

*Note:* Status is as of October 29, 2019. AfCFTA = African Continental Free Trade Area.

tariff and nontariff barriers (NTBs) in goods. This study extends the analysis to cover NTBs in services and other sectors and trade facilitation measures. Most important, the analysis also investigates the implications of AfCFTA for poverty and income distribution and its impacts on unskilled workers, youth, and women.

The forward-looking policy scenarios were designed by employing the global dynamic CGE model and the global microsimulation framework Global Income Distribution Dynamics (GIDD).[3] This approach allows analysis of global development and structural transformation, incorporating the complex interactions of productivity differences at the country, sector, or factor level; shifts in demand as income rises; demographic and skill dynamics in factor markets; and changes in comparative advantage and trade flows from globalization or trade liberalization. Analysis of the distributional outcomes of AfCFTA requires (1) building a new data set on employment

**Figure 1.2**   Trade, GDP, and population of African continent as share of global total

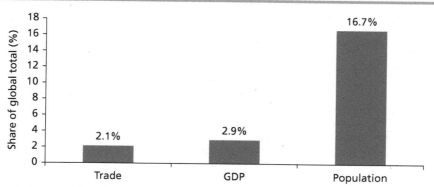

*Source:* World Bank's World Development Indicators (https://datacatalog.worldbank.org/dataset/world
-development-indicators).

*Note:* GDP = gross domestic product.

and wages of female and male workers at the industry level across AfCFTA members;
(2) building a gender-sensitive CGE model; and (3) updating several household
surveys to be used in the microsimulations (see appendix A on the preparation data
on disaggregated labor volumes and wages).

Although in Africa several subregional integration agreements aim in part to
achieve the same set of goals, the impact of AfCFTA is likely to stem from two main
features. First, in the policy areas already covered by subregional agreements, AfCFTA
will provide a nondiscriminatory reduction in tariffs and a common regulatory framework, thereby reducing fragmentation of the continental market. Second, subregional
agreements in Africa tend to be relatively shallow, covering few of the nontariff measures that affect trade integration. AfCFTA could make substantial progress in ensuring
that NTBs are more conducive to continental trade integration. Specifically, to assess
the implications of AfCFTA, the study team develops a set of policy scenarios to cover
(1) tariff changes differentiating between the time frame of tariff liberalization of the
least developed countries (LDCs) and non-LDCs; (2) the reduction of NTBs in goods
and services; and (3) improvements in trade facilitation.

This report begins by presenting background information on the content of
AfCFTA and the data used for the quantification exercise. It then describes the key
findings of the macroeconomic simulations and the analysis of the distributional
impacts of the agreement.

## NOTES

1.  These statistics do not include informal or small-scale cross-border trade flows, which provide
    income for an estimated 43 percent of Africa's population (Afrika and Ajumbo 2012), support
    poverty reduction, and improve food security.

2. GTAP is a global network of researchers and policy makers who conduct quantitative analysis of international policy issues. GTAP is coordinated by the Center for Global Trade Analysis in the Department of Agricultural Economics at Purdue University.

3. See appendix B for a summary description of the GIDD model.

## REFERENCE

Afrika, Jean-Guy K., and Gerald Ajumbo. 2012. "Informal Cross Border Trade in Africa: Implications and Policy Recommendations." *Africa Economic Brief* 3 (10): 13. http://scholar.google.com /scholar?hl=en&btnG=Search&q=intitle:Informal+Cross+Border+Trade+in+Africa:+Implications +and+Policy+Recommendations#3.

# 2 The Content of AfCFTA and African Subregional Trade Agreements

At its launch, the framework agreement establishing the African Continental Free Trade Area (AfCFTA) was signed by 44 countries at a summit of the African Union (AU) held in Kigali, Rwanda, March 21, 2018. AfCFTA was proposed in 2012,[1] and it was hoped that an agreement would be reached by 2017. The first phase comprised negotiation of three protocols: Trade in Goods,[2] Trade in Services,[3] and Rules and Procedures for Settlement of Disputes.

The agreement requires members to progressively remove tariffs on at least 97 percent of tariff lines that account for 90 percent of intra-Africa imports.[4] Average tariffs are 6.1 percent, but with high variation across countries and sectors. Intra-Africa trade is highly concentrated, with 1 percent of tariff lines accounting for 74 percent of imports in the average African country. Thus some of the most onerous and protectionist tariffs may be maintained even if countries liberalize most tariff lines. Trade in certain sensitive sectors is expected to be liberalized over a longer period, but other goods are likely to remain excluded from liberalization.[5]

The AfCFTA annex on rules of origin has not yet been finalized. Rules of origin describe the transformation a product must undergo in the region—such as the share of value added—to enjoy preferential market access. They are used to prevent goods from nonmember countries entering through a low-tariff country and being transshipped duty-free to another member country. Rules of origin that are too restrictive can negate the preferential market access intended by the free trade agreement and prevent global supply chains from functioning. South Africa and Nigeria have expressed concerns that rules of origin too lenient or mismanaged will provoke a flood of extraregional products with low levels of value added.

Negotiations on services began in June 2018, and countries have identified five priority sectors: financial services, transport, telecom/information technology, professional services, and tourism. The benefits of services liberalization extend far beyond the service sectors themselves; they affect all other economic activities in which services are inputs. A second phase of negotiations will focus on investment, competition, and intellectual property rights, with the potential of deepening AfCFTA. Research finds that deep trade agreements boost trade, foreign investment, and participation in global value chains (Laget et al. 2018; Mattoo, Mulabdic, and Ruta 2017; Mulabdic, Osnago, and Ruta 2017). And yet these areas also involve complex negotiations.

An important question is how AfCFTA will complement Africa's subregional preferential trade agreements (PTAs). This analysis compares the legal text of AfCFTA (as signed in March 2018) with the policy areas covered in existing PTAs.[6] It indicates that AfCFTA could promote regional economic integration in Africa in two ways. First, in the policy areas already covered by subregional PTAs, AfCFTA will offer a common regulatory framework, thereby reducing market fragmentation created by different sets of rules. Second, Africa's subregional trade agreements tend to be shallow. AfCFTA will be an opportunity to regulate policy areas important for economic integration that are often regulated in trade agreements but that so far have not been covered in most of Africa's PTAs.

This analysis focuses on the following subregional PTAs, which are in force and were notified to the World Trade Organization (WTO) as of September 2019: Common Market for East and South Africa (COMESA), East African Community (EAC), Economic Community of West African States (ECOWAS), South African Development Community (SADC), South African Customs Union (SACU), West African Economic and Monetary Union (WAEMU), and Economic and Monetary Community of Central Africa (CEMAC).[7] Detailed references to the legal texts of the agreements appear in appendix C.

Understanding the detailed content of trade agreements beyond tariffs is essential to appreciate their potential effects. Modern-day PTAs are not just the more common instruments of trade policy liberalization; countries participating in PTAs have deepened and expanded their scope.[8] The average PTA in the 1950s covered eight policy areas. In recent years, that number went up to 17. "Deep" trade agreements matter for economic development. The rules embedded in these agreements contribute to determining how economies function and grow. For example, trade and investment regimes determine the extent of economic integration; competition rules affect economic efficiency; and intellectual property rights protections matter for innovation.

The inclusion of new policy areas in PTAs is not random. As shown by Mattoo, Mulabdic, and Ruta (2017), trade agreements covering few policy areas generally focus on traditional trade policy areas such as tariff liberalization or customs. Agreements with broader coverage tend to include trade-related regulatory issues such as technical barriers to trade or subsidies. Finally, agreements with large numbers of provisions often include policy areas that are not directly related to trade such as labor, environment, and migration issues.[9] This analysis of the content of AfCFTA and Africa's subregional PTAs focuses on the 20 policy areas most commonly included in trade agreements in force and notified to the WTO.

Two policy areas have largely not been covered in Africa's subregional PTAs but are included in AfCFTA. Intellectual property rights are covered in only one subregional PTA (EAC), and no subregional PTA covers state trading enterprises (STEs).

Table 2.1 Overview of policy areas covered in Africa's subregional PTAs and AfCFTA

| | East African Community (EAC) | Common Market for East and South Africa (COMESA) | South African Development Community (SADC) | Economic Community of West African States (ECOWAS) | West African Economic and Monetary Union (WAEMU) | South African Customs Union (SACU) | Economic and Monetary Community of Central Africa (CEMAC) | African Continental Free Trade Area (AfCFTA) |
|---|---|---|---|---|---|---|---|---|
| Tariffs on manufactured goods | ✓ | ✓ | ✓ | ✓ | ✓ | ✓ | ✓ | ✓ |
| Tariffs on agricultural goods | ✓ | ✓ | ✓ | ✓ | ✓ | ✓ | ✓ | ✓ |
| Export taxes | × | ✓ | ✓ | × | ✓ | × | ✓ | ✓ |
| Customs | ✓ | ✓ | ✓ | ✓ | × | ✓ | × | ✓ |
| Competition policy | ✓ | ✓ | ✓ | × | ✓ | × | ✓ | ✓ |
| State aid | ✓ | ✓ | ✓ | × | × | × | ✓ | ✓ |
| Antidumping | × | ✓ | ✓ | ✓ | × | × | ✓ | ✓ |
| Countervailing measures | × | ✓ | × | ✓ | × | × | × | ✓ |
| STEs | × | × | ✓ | × | × | × | × | ✓ |
| TBTs | ✓ | ✓ | ✓ | ✓ | ✓ | × | ✓ | ✓ |
| GATS | ✓ | ✓ | ✓ | ✓ | × | × | ✓ | ✓ |
| SPS measures | ✓ | ✓ | ✓ | ✓ | ✓ | × | ✓ | ✓ |
| Movement of capital | ✓ | ✓ | × | ✓ | × | × | ✓ | ✓ |
| Public procurement | ✓ | × | × | × | × | × | × | × |
| IPRs | ✓ | × | × | × | × | × | × | ✓ |
| Investment | ✓ | ✓ | ✓ | × | × | × | × | ✓ |
| Environmental laws | ✓ | ✓ | × | ✓ | × | × | ✓ | × |
| Labor market regulations | ✓ | ✓ | × | × | × | × | × | × |

*Source:* Based on Hofmann, Osnago, and Ruta (2017).

*Note:* ✓ = policy area covered; × = policy area not covered; AfCFTA = African Continental Free Trade Area; GATS = General Agreement on Trade in Services; IPRs = intellectual property rights; PTAs = preferential trade agreements; SPS = sanitary and phytosanitary; STEs = state trading enterprises; TBTs = technical barriers to trade.

Finally, although AfCFTA is deeper than any of the existing subregional PTAs, some policy areas are included in individual subregional PTAs but not in AfCFTA (table 2.1). Examples of these areas are state aid (subsidies),[10] environmental laws,[11] labor market regulations,[12] and public procurement.[13] The exclusion of these policy areas in AfCFTA does not prevent countries from aiming for common regulations at a later stage and does not affect the commitments made by countries in the context of the subregional PTAs.

An important issue is how inconsistencies or conflict between different jurisdictions, subregional or regional, will be addressed. As a general comment, Article 19 of the AfCFTA treaty refers to "conflict and inconsistency with Regional Agreements." Article 19(1) establishes that, unless otherwise provided, AfCFTA prevails in cases of inconsistencies. At the same time, Article 19(2) refers to "higher levels of regional integration" than those established in AfCFTA, such as in "regional economic communities, regional trading arrangements and custom unions." In the latter situation, and as a general rule, parties maintain such higher levels among themselves. It remains to be seen how this will be implemented in practice.

## NOTES

1.  African Union Assembly Decision Assembly/AU/Dec. 394 (XVIII) as part of the Action Plan on Boosting Intra-Africa Trade (BIAT).

2.  The overarching aims of the agreement for goods are (1) progressively eliminating tariffs; (2) progressively eliminating nontariff barriers; (3) enhancing the efficiency of customs, trade facilitation, and transit; (4) promoting cooperation on technical barriers to trade (TBTs) and sanitary and phytosanitary (SPS) measures; (5) developing and promoting regional and continental value chains; and (6) promoting socioeconomic development, diversification, and industrialization across Africa.

3.  The overarching aims of the agreement for services are (1) enhancing competitiveness of services; (2) promoting sustainable development; (3) fostering investment; (4) accelerating efforts in industrial development to promote the development of regional value chains; and (5) progressively liberalizing trade in services.

4.  A special dispensation for seven least developed countries has also been tabled, providing for a reduced level of ambition on tariff liberalization. At entry into force of AfCFTA, Djibouti, Ethiopia, Madagascar, Malawi, Sudan, Zambia, and Zimbabwe will be expected to meet a reduced level of ambition of 85 percent of tariffs, with a 15-year period to reach 90 percent.

5.  AfCFTA would benefit from the lessons produced by the World Bank's most recent analysis of trade policy and barriers in the Economic and Monetary Community of Central Africa (CEMAC). Fiess et al. (2018) finds that trade within CEMAC remains limited despite a significant regional integration effort.

6.  The analysis of the subregional PTAs draws on the World Bank's database on the content of trade agreements (Hofmann, Osnago, and Ruta 2017). This database is based on a review of policy areas covered in each PTA's main legal instrument or founding treaty.

7.  Not included in this analysis are four regional economic communities (RECs) recognized by the AfCFTA agreement but are not trade agreements that have been notified to the WTO: Arab Maghreb Union (UMA); Community of Sahel-Saharan States (CEN-SAD); Economic Community of Central African States (ECCAS); and Intergovernmental Authority on Development (IGAD). SACU, WAEMU, and CEMAC are not acknowledged as RECs in the AfCFTA agreement (Article 1(t)) but fall within the ambit of Article 19(2) of the AfCFTA treaty.

8. Preferential trade agreements have always been a feature of the world trading system, but their prominence has changed in recent years. The number of PTAs increased from 50 in the early 1990s to roughly 300 in 2019. All WTO members are currently party to at least one PTA and often several.

9. A study of European Union and U.S. trade agreements identified 52 potential policy areas covered in PTAs (Horn, Mavroidis, and Sapir 2010).

10. EAC, COMESA, SADC, and CEMAC.

11. EAC, COMESA, ECOWAS, and CEMAC.

12. EAC and COMESA.

13. EAC.

## REFERENCES

Fiess, Norbert Matthias, Aguera, Philippe Marie Aquera, Cesar Calderon, Leif Jensen, Joanne Catherine Gaskell, John C. Keyser, Hannah Sibylle Nielsen, Alberto Portugal, and Jose E. Signoret. 2018. *Deepening Regional Integration to Advance Growth and Prosperity.* Washington, DC: World Bank Group. http://documents.worldbank.org/curated/en/491781560455916201/Deepening-Regional-Integration-to-Advance-Growth-and-Prosperity.

Hofmann, Claudia, Alberto Osnago, and Michele Ruta. 2017. "Horizontal Depth: A New Database on the Content of Preferential Trade Agreements." Policy Research Working Paper 7981, World Bank, Washington, DC.

Horn, Henrik, Petros C. Mavroidis, and André Sapir. 2010. "Beyond the WTO? An Anatomy of EU and US Preferential Trade Agreements." *World Economy* 33 (11): 1565–88. https://doi.org/10.1111/j.1467-9701.2010.01273.x.

Laget, Edith, Alberto Osnago, Nadia Rocha, and Michele Ruta. 2018. "Deep Agreements and Global Value Chains." Policy Research Working Paper 8491, World Bank, Washington, DC.

Mattoo, Aaditya, Alen Mulabdic, and Michele Ruta. 2017. "Trade Creation and Trade Diversion in Deep Agreements." Policy Research Working Paper 8206, World Bank, Washington, DC.

Mulabdic, Alen, Alberto Osnago, and Michele Ruta. 2017. "Deep Integration and UK–EU Trade Relations." Policy Research Working Paper 7947, World Bank, Washington, DC.

# 3 Literature Review

The results of this analysis are broadly in line with the existing literature on the quantitative impacts of the African Continental Free Trade Area (AfCFTA). All studies conducted so far have focused on evaluating the implications of reductions in tariffs and nontariff barriers (NTBs), as well as of trade facilitation measures, on African welfare. The studies are reviewed in appendix D (recent World Bank research on regional integration in Africa is summarized in appendix E).

Table 3.1 summarizes the key findings of studies incorporating the computable general equilibrium (CGE) and structural trade models in terms of the economic growth and trade implications of AfCFTA. Despite the fact that all previous CGE

**Table 3.1** Summary of key findings from literature review

*percent*

| | Scenario | GDP | GDP, African trade | Total exports | Total imports |
|---|---|---|---|---|---|
| *Removal of tariffs on intra-AfCFTA trade* | | | | | |
| ADB (2019) | Removal of all tariffs on intra-AfCFTA trade | 0.10 (US$2.8 billion) | 14.60 (US$10.1 billion) | 1.00 (US$5.8 billion) | 0.90 (US$5.8 billion) |
| Mevel and Karingi (2012) | Removal of all tariffs on intra-AfCFTA trade by 2017 + CET | 0.20 | 52.30 | 4.00 | |
| Jensen and Sandrey (2015) | Removal of all tariffs on intra-AfCFTA trade | 0.70 | 4.30 | 3.11 | |
| Saygili, Peters, and Knebel (2018) | Removal of all tariffs on intra-AfCFTA trade | 0.97 | 32.80 | 2.50 | 1.80 |
| Abrego et al. (2019) | Removal of all import tariffs | 0.037– 0.053[a] | | | |
| This analysis | Gradual removal of 97% of tariffs on intra-AfCFTA trade | 0.13 (US$12 billion) | 21.76 (US$131 billion) | 1.78 (US$35 billion) | 2.31 (US$41 billion) |

*continued*

**Table 3.1**    Summary of key findings from literature review *(continued)*

| | Scenario | GDP | GDP, African trade | Total exports | Total imports |
|---|---|---|---|---|---|
| **Removal of tariffs and NTBs on intra-AfCFTA trade** | | | | | |
| ADB (2019) | Removal of all tariffs on intra-AfCFTA trade; removal of NTBs | 1.25 (US$37 billion) | 107.20 (US$74.3 billion) | 44.30 (US$107.2 billion) | 33.80 (US$214.1 billion) |
| Jensen and Sandrey (2015) | Removal of all tariffs on intra-AfCFTA trade; 50% reduction in NTBs | 1.60 | 7.26 | 6.28 | |
| Abrego et al. (2019) | Removal of all tariffs; 35% reduction in NTBs | 7.60–1.89–2.11[a] | 8.40 | | |
| This analysis | Gradual removal of 97% of tariffs on intra-AfCFTA trade | 2.24 | 51.85 | 18.84 | 19.58 |
| **Removal of tariffs and NTBs on intra-AfCFTA trade and implementation of TFA** | | | | | |
| ADB (2019) | Removal of all tariffs on intra-AfCFTA trade; removal of NTBs; implementation of TFA | 3.50 (US$100 billion) | 132.70 (US$92 billion) | 51.10 (US$295.6 billion) | 46.20 (US$292.8 billion) |
| This analysis | Gradual removal of 97% of tariffs on intra-AfCFTA trade; 50% reduction in NTBs; implementation of TFA | 4.20 (US$413 billion) | 92.07 (US$556 billion) | 28.64 (US$560 billion) | 40.61 (US$714 billion) |

*Source:* World Bank study team.

*Note:* AfCFTA = African Continental Free Trade Area; CET = common external tariff; GDP = gross domestic product; NTB = nontariff barrier; TFA = trade facilitation agreement.

a. Equivalent valuation.

studies apply comparative static simulations and are based on older data sets—the Gobal Trade Analysis Project (GTAP) version 9 or earlier—and often more aggressive trade liberalization scenarios—such as full tariff liberalization and full elimination of NTBs—the results of this analysis are broadly aligned. Consistently, the biggest gains are expected from the reduction of NTBs and from trade facilitation, with significant increases in intra-Africa trade of between 50 and 132 percent and gross domestic product (GDP) gains of between 1 and 4 percent.

## REFERENCES

Abrego, Lisandro, Maria Alejandra Amado, Tunc Gursoy, Garth Nicholls, and Hector Perez-Saiz. 2019. "The African Continental Free Trade Agreement: Welfare Gains Estimates from a General Equilibrium Model." https://www.imf.org/en/Publications/WP/Issues/2019/06/07/The-African -Continental-Free-Trade-Agreement-Welfare-Gains-Estimates-from-a-General-46881.

ADB (African Development Bank). 2019. *African Economic Outlook 2019*. Abidjan, Côte d'Ivoire: ADB.

Jensen, Has Grinsted, and Ron Sandrey. 2015. *The Continental Free Trade Area: A GTAP Assessment*. South Africa: Trade Law Centre.

Mevel, Simon, and Stephen Karingi. 2012. "Deepening Regional Integration in Africa: A Computer General Equilibrium Assessment of the Establishment of a Continental Free Trade Area Followed by a Continental Customs Union." United Nations Economic Commission for Africa, Addis Ababa, Ethiopia.

Saygili, Mesut, Ralf Peters, and Christian Knebel. 2018. "African Continental Free Trade Area: Challenges and Opportunities of Tariff Reductions." Research Paper No. 15, United Nations Conference on Trade and Development (UNCTAD), Geneva, Switzerland.

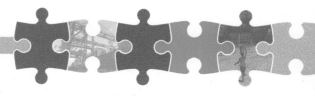

# **4** Data and Methodology

## DATA

The core data for this study are taken from the Global Trade Analysis Project (GTAP) database (Aguiar et al. 2019)—see appendix F. The data provide a snapshot of the global economy in 2014, including domestic interindustry flows and bilateral trade flows. The full database covers 141 regions, of which 121 are individual countries, and 65 sectors. For the purposes of this study, the 141 regions are aggregated into 37 regions, including all 32 regions in Africa that are part of the database. Of those 32 regions, 24 are individual countries, with the remaining countries aggregated into five regional components.[1] The 65 sectors are aggregated into 21 sectors. The GTAP data are based on official trade flows, but the magnitude of small-scale cross-border trade (SSCBT) is estimated to be substantial in Africa (box 4.1), leading to underestimation of the actual trade flows.

The core data are supplemented with additional information. GTAP's tariff rates are replaced with the most recent estimates, as measured by the World Bank. In addition, the study incorporates estimates of nontariff trade barriers (NTBs). The NTBs for goods are sourced from World Bank's World Integrated Trade Solution (WITS) database and documented by Kee, Nicita, and Olarreaga (2009). They are aggregated to the model's regional and sector aggregation using trade weights. Estimates for the missing countries and regions are simple averages of the available estimates. The NTBs for services are sourced from Jafari and Tarr (2015). These are provided for 11 services that are mapped to an aggregation of GTAP services. These three sources of data are incorporated into the 2014 reference year using a procedure that aims to preserve as much as possible the original structure of the aggregated GTAP database.

## GLOBAL DYNAMIC COMPUTABLE GENERAL EQUILIBRIUM MODEL

The quantitative estimates of the impacts of the African Continental Free Trade Area (AfCFTA) rely on the Envisage computable general equilibrium (CGE) model (appendix G). This recursive dynamic model, calibrated to the GTAP database, has been used by the World Bank in a number of studies.[2] The baseline, or reference simulation, runs from 2014 through 2035. The simulation is calibrated to the United Nations population projection (2015 revision), combined with a long-term socioeconomic scenario developed by the Integrated Assessment Modeling (IAM) community—the so-called socioeconomic pathways (SSPs). Five such pathways describe possible storylines of the evolution of the global gross domestic product (GDP). SSP2, the Middle of the Road Scenario, was selected for this study.

## DISTRIBUTIONAL IMPACTS OF AfCFTA

The poverty and distributional impacts of AfCFTA depend on the changes in relative prices across and within countries. To capture the full—both between and within a country—distributional change, one needs a framework that captures effects at the macro level (country averages) and the evolution of factor markets at the micro level (dispersion). To account for both effects, this study uses the Global Income Distribution Dynamics (GIDD) microsimulation framework in combination with the Envisage global CGE model (see appendix A).[3] Both tools have been developed at the World Bank and are described in detail by Bourguignon, Bussolo, and Pereira da Silva (2008); Bussolo, De Hoyos, and Medvedev (2010); and van der Mensbrugghe (2013). The sections that follow briefly describe features of the GIDD framework.

### Employment volume and remuneration, gender, and skill

Detailed labor statistics by gender and skill are needed to assess the economic impacts of AfCFTA beyond its macroeconomic aggregates, thereby deepening the capacity of the CGE model to account for and draw conclusions about employment and its remuneration for specific segments of the population such as women and youth. Additional labor market information is incorporated for each country and activity in the GTAP version 10 database. The initial levels of employment as of 2014 with average remuneration (in U.S. dollars) are for four different types of workers who are differentiated based on their gender (male and female) and educational attainment (skilled and unskilled)—see table 4.1 later in this chapter. These statistics were constructed using harmonized nationally representative household surveys available from the World Bank and the Luxembourg Income Study. Because of the natural inconsistency between macro- and microbased statistics, adjustments were performed so that total volumes and wages added up to national accounts.

This procedure is explained in detail in appendix B. Figure 4.1 summarizes in a box and whisker plot the initial distribution of female employment by economic activity for AfCFTA countries. On the horizontal axis, a value of female labor intensity greater than 1 indicates that an economic activity employs a greater proportion of women than the rest of the economy.[4] Across Africa, the economic activities that tend to employ more women are those in services (recreational and other, insurance, real estate, trade, and financial) and the textiles and wearing apparel sector.

**Box 4.1    The importance of small-scale cross-border trade in Africa**

Although deeper regional integration is one of the key trade policy objectives for countries in Africa, a large part of intra-Africa trade currently goes unrecorded. Cross-border transactions often take place on a small scale, and so such consignments are not captured by the standard statistical recording of trade through customs declarations. Because the number of small shipments can be very large, the total unrecorded volume and value of trade can be substantial. Thus official trade statistics are incomplete and possibly misleading.

Indeed, the poor quality of official trade statistics is one reason the recorded regional trade in Africa remains surprisingly low (Golub 2015). For example, the Petite-Barriere border crossing between Rwanda and the Democratic Republic of Congo in Goma is one of the busiest borders in Africa, with more than 40,000 small-scale traders crossing on a normal day. Because of the poor official trade statistics, policy makers lack the complete understanding of the magnitude of the impediments to intraregional trade required to design effective trade and investment policies.

These unrecorded cross-border transactions are sometimes casually referred to as "informal trade" or "illegal trade." Although many small-scale traders may not be registered as formal business owners, their informal status does not imply that they are intentionally trying to circumvent the existing laws, applicable taxes, or relevant procedures (Brenton and Soprano 2018). Moreover, some individuals may conduct both formal and informal activities, pay one tax and not another, or complete one formality and not another (WCO 2015).

Previous research has revealed that small-scale traders and the producers and consumers with whom they connect fall into the bottom third of the population by household income. Thus the small-scale cross-border trade is directly relevant to poverty reduction (Brenton, Gamberoni, and Sear 2013). In addition, SSCBT also makes a notable contribution to regional food security by linking markets across borders.

A large proportion of small-scale operators at border crossings tend to be female. Women assume a variety of roles in small-scale trade as border traders, transporters, processors, or vendors. Often, they face more severe impediments to trade than their male colleagues in the form of higher trade costs and more pervasive corruption, more limited access to price and market information, and more frequent harassment and abuse (Aboudou et al. 2017; Brenton, Gamberoni, and Sear 2013).

A range of studies based on surveys at borders attest to the importance of small-sale trade across a range of countries in Africa. For example, Mitaritonna, Bensassi, and Jarreau (2018) analyze data from interviews with 8,883 traders at border crossings from Benin to Togo and Nigeria. They find that unrecorded imports into Benin are as important as recorded imports, and for exports the value of unrecorded transactions are more than five times higher than the official exports reported in customs statistics.

The statistical offices of Uganda and Rwanda have been monitoring the quantitative and qualitative aspects of SSCBT since 2005 and 2010, respectively. These efforts serve as the most rigorous and reliable assessments of the importance of SSCBT. Uganda sends enumerators to targeted borders for two weeks a month to capture SSCBT trade flows through observation and then to extrapolate the data for full-month coverage. Rwanda uses enumerators recruited in the border areas who, equipped with electronic tablets, administer a survey throughout the year. In both countries, the observed SSCBT has been substantial. In 2017 almost 16 percent (US$550 million) of Uganda's total exports were attributable to small-scale trade, but at the regional level almost 30 percent of Uganda's exports to neighbors were SSCBT. About 60 percent of Uganda's exports to the Democratic Republic of Congo consists of SSCBT. Similarly, for Rwanda about 11 percent of total exports is based on small-scale trade, rising to 45 percent for exports to neighbors. More than half of Rwanda's imports from Burundi and a quarter of imports from the Democratic Republic of Congo arise from small-scale trade.

The magnitude and importance of small-scale trade in Africa suggest that policy reforms such as AfCFTA should address the extensive barriers to such trade. If they are addressed, the increase in regional trade will be substantially higher than is predicted by using officially recorded trade data.

*Source:* Based on Aggarwal, Hoppe, and Walkenhorst (2019).

**Figure 4.1**  Female employment intensity in disaggregated labor database, AfCFTA countries

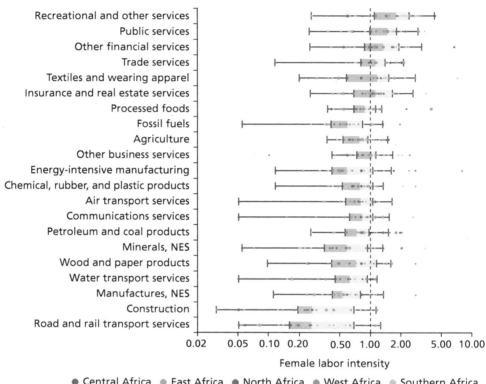

*Source:* Estimates, World Bank study team.

*Note:* AfCFTA = African Continental Free Trade Area; NES = not elsewhere specified.

By contrast, women tend to be employed the least in construction, mining, and road and rail transport services. Although this finding is true in general, the box and whisker plot show also that there is significant variation in female labor intensity across the African continent.

The second set of data complementing the CGE model are related to the expected formation of skills in each country. Projections for the working-age population by gender, five-year age groups, and educational attainment are incorporated into the CGE model. These series are in line with the initial labor volumes, with population totals from the United Nations' *World Population Prospects 2019* (UN DESA 2019), assuming constant enrollment ratios for educational progress. The demographic and skill formation implications for AfCFTA countries are summarized in figure 4.2. The figure shows the formation of skills in North Africa compared with Sub-Saharan Africa beginning with the implementation of AfCFTA in 2020 until the simulation target year, 2035. By 2035, employment in North Africa is expected to grow from 64.2 million to 75.9 million, at an annual rate of increase of 1.12 percent, which is very close to the average of the non-AfCFTA

**Figure 4.2** Projected employment by gender and skill: North Africa and Sub-Saharan Africa, 2020 and 2035

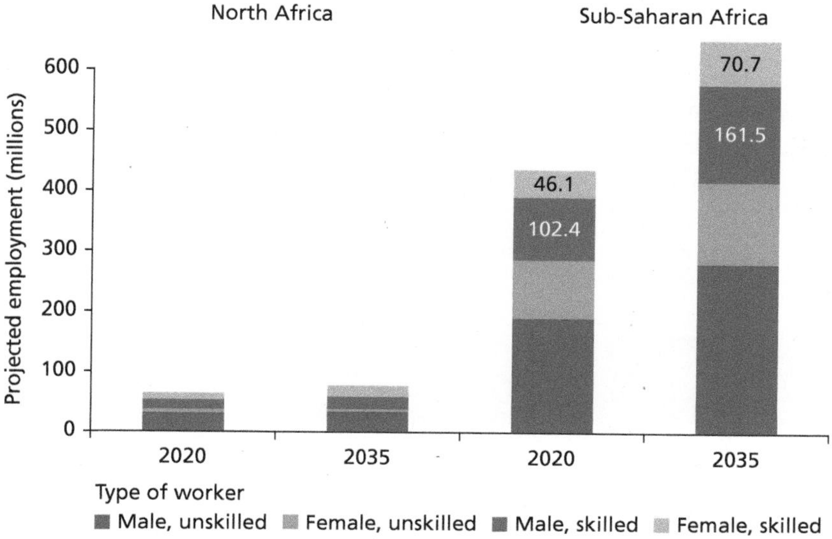

Source: Estimates, World Bank study team.

countries (not shown in the graph). By contrast, Sub-Saharan Africa's employment is expected to grow from 437 million to more than 650 million, at an annual rate of increase of 2.7 percent. In absolute terms, the number of educated (skilled) workers would grow by nearly 92 million, at an annual rate of increase of 2.83 percent.

Table 4.1 summarizes in relative terms the information on initial employment for the four categories of workers (gender and skill). The information is presented according to the aggregation of activities used in this study. In 2014, the base year of the simulation, agriculture is the largest employer in Africa by sector with 38.5 percent of total employment, followed by trade and public services. In fact, two out of every three jobs in Africa are in the group formed by (1) agriculture; (2) wholesale and retail trade, accommodation, and food services (trade); and (3) education, health, electricity, water, and public sector (public services). At the continental level, the manufacturing sector accounts for 12.6 percent of employment, of which 42 percent is in food processing.

The participation of women is 31.9 percent continent-wide, but services tend to employ a larger proportion. For example, women as a percentage of labor in recreational services is 49.7 percent; in air transport, 42.0 percent; and in public services, 40.4 percent. Some industries attract fewer women, such as construction (13.2 percent); road and rail transport services (12.5 percent); and minerals, not elsewhere specified (25.8 percent). Textiles and wearing apparel is above the average at 33.4 percent, masked by large variations across countries, as discussed earlier.

At the continental level, skilled employment represents 33.8 percent of total employment. Skilled employees are defined as individuals with more than nine years of schooling in low- and lower-middle-income countries and more than 12 years of schooling in upper-middle- and high-income countries. The more sophisticated services tend to employ a larger share of skilled workers, such as other financial services (65.2 percent), air transport (57.5 percent), and insurance and real estate (56.3 percent), with an equally large proportion of skilled employment in public services (64.4 percent). Agriculture (16.3 percent) and fossil fuels (24.7 percent) employ a lower proportion of skilled labor.

In the observed wage differentials by gender (females with respect to males) and by skill (skilled with respect to unskilled) reported in table 4.1, the wages for females are 23.4 percent lower than those for males, particularly in the sectors of

**Table 4.1**   Employment and wages in Africa, initial simulation parameters

*percent*

| Activity | Employment | | | Wage premium | |
|---|---|---|---|---|---|
| | Total | Females | Skilled | Females | Skilled |
| Agriculture | 38.5 | 30.8 | 16.3 | −38.4 | 40.2 |
| Fossil fuels | 2.2 | 33.0 | 24.7 | −20.6 | 95.0 |
| Minerals, NES | 0.5 | 25.8 | 29.7 | −44.1 | 47.5 |
| Processed foods | 6.0 | 32.8 | 31.3 | −40.2 | 58.7 |
| Wood and paper products | 0.8 | 25.7 | 31.8 | −31.7 | 57.1 |
| Textiles and wearing apparel | 1.7 | 33.4 | 35.6 | −27.1 | 41.2 |
| Energy-intensive manufacturing | 1.8 | 27.0 | 32.0 | −42.1 | 32.5 |
| Petroleum and coal products | 0.1 | 26.3 | 23.4 | −25.3 | 88.9 |
| Chemical, rubber, and plastic products | 0.8 | 27.6 | 32.7 | −39.8 | 38.3 |
| Manufactures, NES | 1.8 | 21.3 | 39.5 | −19.0 | 30.4 |
| Construction | 3.8 | 13.2 | 39.3 | −37.9 | 160.7 |
| Trade services | 15.5 | 34.2 | 40.3 | −26.7 | 129.8 |
| Road and rail transport services | 2.0 | 12,.5 | 41.2 | −2.0 | 69.9 |
| Water transport services | 0.2 | 21.6 | 55.1 | −9.2 | 28.6 |
| Air transport services | 0.3 | 42.0 | 57.5 | −45.9 | 40.5 |
| Communication services | 2.6 | 27.1 | 50.3 | −14.2 | 73.8 |
| Other financial services | 1.6 | 35.2 | 65.2 | −3.3 | 44.4 |
| Insurance and real estate services | 0.7 | 34.4 | 56.3 | 5.6 | 38.0 |
| Other business services | 2.9 | 30.3 | 46.1 | −15.9 | 75.3 |
| Recreational services | 2.3 | 49.7 | 31.0 | −20.5 | 42.6 |
| Public services | 13.7 | 40.4 | 64.4 | −11.0 | 45.7 |
| Africa, total | 100.0 | 31.9 | 33.8 | −23.4 | 105.7 |

*Source:* Estimates, World Bank study team.

*Note:* NES = not elsewhere specified.

minerals (−44.1 percent), air transport (−45.9 percent), and agriculture (−38.4 percent). In the database, females are reported to earn comparatively higher wages by weighted average in a few industries such as insurance and real estate services (5.6 percent). The skill premia across the continent is 105.7 percent and higher for construction (160.7 percent), trade services (129.8 percent), and fossil fuels (95 percent).

## Scenario assumptions

The AfCFTA scenario relies on three specific instruments:

1. Tariffs on intracontinental trade are progressively reduced in line with AfCFTA modalities. Starting in 2020, tariffs on 90 percent of tariff lines will be eliminated over a five-year period (10-year period for the least developed countries, or LDCs). Starting in 2025, tariffs on an additional 7 percent of tariff lines will be eliminated over a five-year period (eight-year period for LDCs). A maximum of 3 percent of tariff lines that account for no more than 10 percent of intra-Africa imports can be excluded from liberalization by the end of 2030 (2033 for LDCs).
2. NTBs on both goods and services are reduced on a most-favored-nation (MFN) basis. It is assumed that 50 percent of NTBs are actionable within the context of AfCFTA—with a cap of 50 percentage points. These are implemented as ad valorem tariff equivalents. It is also assumed that reduction of NTBs benefits African exporters to non-AfCFTA markets with an additional reduction of NTBs by 20 percent.
3. AfCFTA will also be accompanied by measures that facilitate trade such as implementation of a trade facilitation agreement (TFA). Estimates of the size of these trade barriers were obtained from a recent study by de Melo and Sorgho (2019). These are halved, although capped at 10 percentage points.

## Tariffs

For most countries, intraregional imports are relatively small, accounting for less than 20 percent of total imports (figure 4.3). For countries with a higher share of intraregional imports, the applied average tariffs on intraregional imports are low because, according to statutory tariff rates, most intraregional trade in these countries is conducted under zero or very low preferential tariffs as part of subregional trade agreements such as the South African Customs Union (SACU) and the South African Development Community (SADC). (For a description of statutory tariff data availability by country, see appendix H.)

Tariff lines are classified into three product categories (nonsensitive, sensitive, and excluded) to minimize tariff revenue losses. Tariff reductions are simulated following the trade liberalization modalities adopted under AfCFTA. Starting in 2020, tariffs on 90 percent of tariff lines (nonsensitive products) will be eliminated over a five-year period (10-year period for LDCs). Starting in 2025, tariffs on an additional 7 percent

**Figure 4.3**   Share of imports and average tariffs imposed on AfCFTA imports

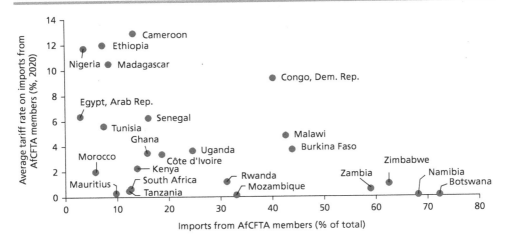

*Source:* Estimates, World Bank study team.

*Note:* Trade weights are based on benchmark trade flows in 2014 GTAP database. AfCFTA = African Continental Free Trade Area; GTAP = Global Trade Analysis Project.

of tariff lines (sensitive products) will be eliminated over a five-year period (eight-year period for LDCs). Three percent of tariff lines that account for no more than 10 percent of intra-Africa imports can be excluded from liberalization by the end of 2030 (2033 for LDCs). The tariff reductions for both sensitive and nonsensitive products are implemented as equal (linear) cuts over their respective liberalization periods.

Tariff lines are ranked in descending order by tariff revenues generated by African imports. The bottom 90 percent of tariff lines are classified as nonsensitive products, the next 7 percent as sensitive products, and the remaining 3 percent as excluded products. However, the list of excluded products includes only the tariff lines with the largest tariff revenues up to a cumulative intraregional import share of 10 percent, and the remaining tariff lines are reclassified as sensitive products. Because tariff revenues are more concentrated than imports, exclusion lists include fewer than 1 percent of tariff lines for most countries.

The lists of excluded products selected according to the methodology are from a wide selection of sectors. No sector clearly dominates the sensitive lists in all countries, although most of the products are from the manufacturing sector: machinery (10 percent), auto (10 percent), apparel (9 percent), chemicals (8 percent), and iron and steel (6 percent). Agricultural products—especially prepared food and beverages (14 percent) and fruits and vegetables (9 percent)—account for about a quarter of products in the sensitive lists. This breakdown considers only the tariff lines included in excluded lists but not the share of imports that they represent.

As a result of AfCFTA, the largest liberalization is expected in countries with high initial barriers such as Cameroon, Nigeria, Ethiopia, Madagascar, Democratic Republic of Congo, and the Arab Republic of Egypt (figures 4.4 and 4.5). From 2020 to 2035,

**Figure 4.4**    Trade-weighted tariffs imposed on AfCFTA imports by country, 2020 and 2035

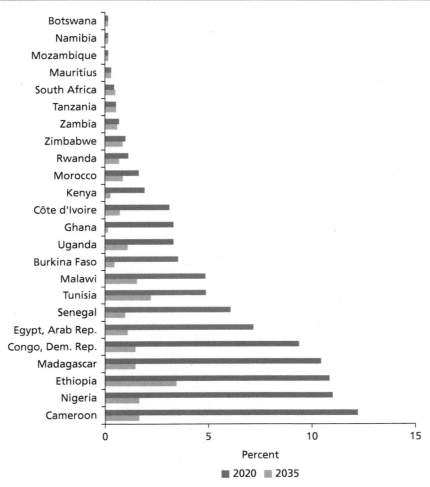

*Source:* Estimates, World Bank study team.

*Note:* AfCFTA = African Continental Free Trade Area.

import tariffs do not decline compared with those for the rest of the world. Average intra-Africa (trade-weighted) tariffs decline from 5.2 percent to 1.4 percent, with the highest declines in manufacturing from 7 percent to 2 percent and in agriculture from 5 to 2 percent (figure 4.5).

## Nontariff barriers

The NTB estimates for goods are sourced from WITS based on the methodology developed by Kee, Nicita, and Olarreaga (2009). The original data at the HS6 level were first aggregated to the 65-sector GTAP level using trade weights (see appendix F). At the continental level, the average trade weight tariffs are at about 5 percent, with the highest tariffs imposed on processed foods, textiles and wearing apparel, and

**Figure 4.5**   Trade-weighted tariffs imposed on AfCFTA imports by sector, 2020 and 2035

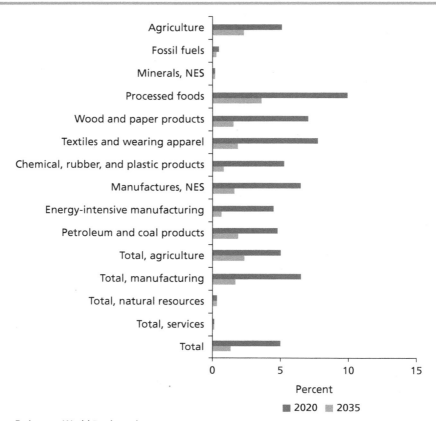

*Source:* Estimates, World Bank study team.

*Note:* AfCFTA = African Continental Free Trade Area; NES = not elsewhere specified.

manufacturing products, not elsewhere specified (NES)—see figure 4.6. The average trade-weighted NTBs for goods and services amount to 30 percent, with the highest levels in manufacturing (37 percent), followed by agriculture (30 percent), natural resources (15 percent), and services (8 percent)—see figure 4.7. The initial barriers to trade in services are much higher (see appendix F), but the study works with trade-weighted averages, which reduces their value quite dramatically. The aggregate numbers again mask the great heterogeneity of the starting value of NTBs by sectors, with some countries registering NTBs as high as 104 percent in insurance and real estate services (Democratic Republic of Congo) to 2 percent for the same sector in Mozambique.

AfCFTA will likely reduce the trade costs associated with NTBs because it creates a common set of rules for participating countries in areas such as competition, technical barriers to trade, and sanitary and phytosanitary standards. Translating reforms in these areas into reductions in trade costs is a difficult task. For the purpose of this study, it is assumed that under the AfCFTA scenario, 50 percent of the NTBs are actionable,

**Figure 4.6**  Trade-weighted nontariff barriers imposed on AfCFTA imports by country, 2020 and 2035

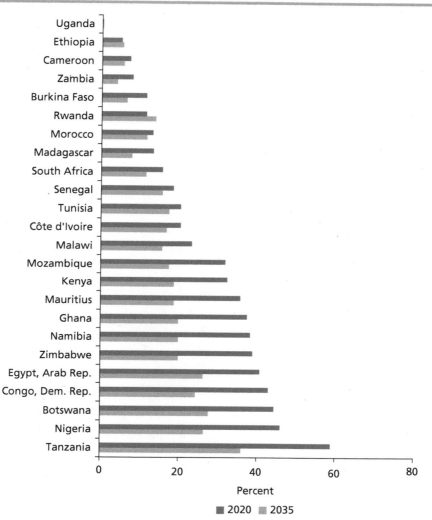

*Source:* Estimates, World Bank study team.

*Note:* AfCFTA = African Continental Free Trade Area.

with a cap of 50 percentage points.[5] This assumption is in line with previous studies on AfCFTA and other deep agreements such as the Trans-Pacific Partnership study by Petri and Plummer (2016). In that study, only a fraction of NTBs are actual barriers that could be actionable (that is, are politically feasible in a trade agreement); the rest are assumed to be beyond the reach of politically viable trade policies. NTBs are implemented as ad valorem tariff equivalents. Under this assumption, there is a sharp drop in NTB ad valorem rates. For intra-Africa trade, the drop is 11.0 percentage points on average, with

**Figure 4.7**   Trade-weighted nontariff barriers imposed on AfCFTA imports by sector, 2020 and 2035

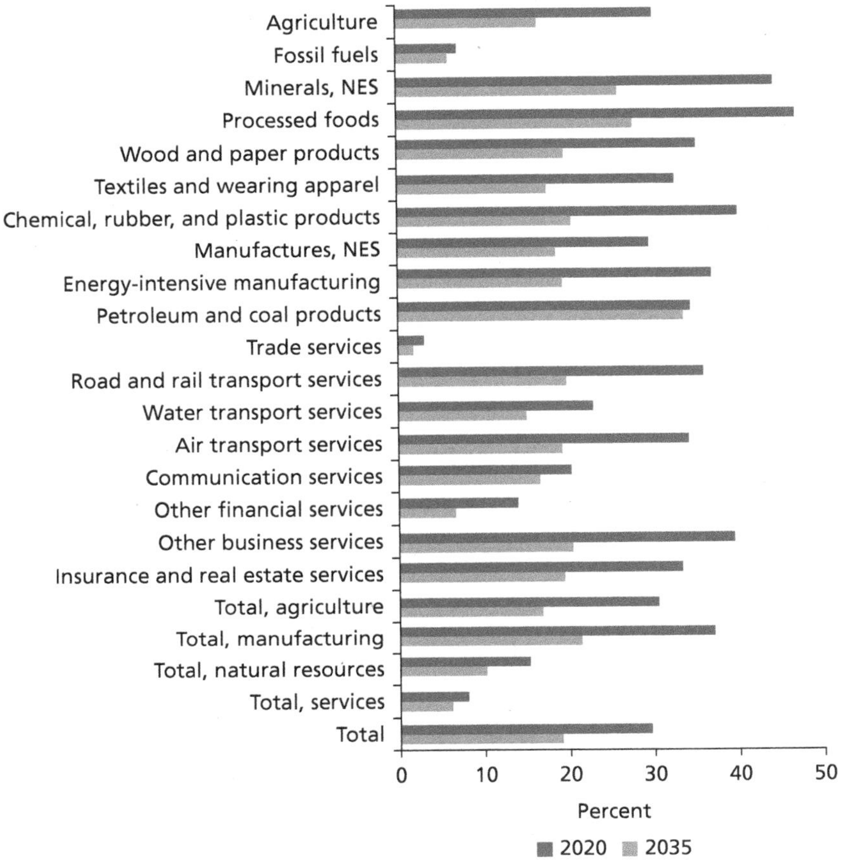

Source: Estimates, World Bank study team.

Note: AfCFTA = African Continental Free Trade Area; NES = not elsewhere specified.

declines of 13.5 percentage points in agriculture and 15.5 in manufacturing. The impact on services is relatively smaller—only 2.0 percentage points.

The NTB changes are assumed to apply to MFN countries—that is, they apply as well to imports from non-Africa countries.[6] The declines in the NTB rates are substantial compared with those of the rest of the world, with an average decline of 13 percentage points—17 points in agriculture, 14 points in manufacturing, and a relatively sizable 8 points in services. It is assumed that the reduction in trade costs associated with NTBs also benefits African exporters to non-AfCFTA markets through domestic measures that reduce the cost of compliance with foreign standards and regulations, with an additional reduction of trade costs associated with NTBs of 20 percent.

## TRADE FACILITATION

By bringing greater attention and policy oversight to trade within Africa, AfCFTA provides an opportunity to improve trade facilitation more widely in the continent at borders and along corridors between African countries. The trade facilitation agreement provides the framework and access to knowledge to guide such improvements, and AfCFTA provides the political momentum and additional commitment mechanism to support broad implementation. Although in certain aspects such as local transit, AfCFTA commitments could go beyond TFA commitments, the TFA could provide stronger mechanisms for implementation of AfCFTA. The benefits of TFA implementation will increase as neighboring countries implement it, and the trade costs along all borders will decrease. In estimating the upper bound of gains, it is assumed that all countries implement the TFA fully as part of AfCFTA process. This estimate is based in turn on the estimates of de Melo and Sorgho (2019), which apply a model that predicts observed time in customs as a function of basic structural variables (GDP, Logistics Performance Index, and Infrastructure Quality Index); policy variables (World Governance Indicators); and the trade facilitation variables captured by the trade facilitation indicator (row L).[7]

After controlling for the structural and policy variables, de Melo and Sorgho (2019) find that a higher trade facilitation indicator score reduces the probability of a longer time in customs. The overall differences in reductions in costs reflect disparities in trade facilitation indicator values and in time in customs for imports. The model provides estimates of the reduction of time in customs that stem from full implementation of the TFA. Those reductions in time are then translated into ad valorem equivalents of barriers using the methodology of Hummels and Schaur (2012), who estimated that one extra day in customs is equivalent to a 1.3 percent extra tariff at the destination based on maritime trade flows to the United States.

The gains from implementing the TFA are simulated by applying the econometric estimates of the ad valorem equivalents of the time lost in customs reported in table 4.2. In the TFA scenario, each African landlocked country takes the average value of the top two landlocked countries in the developing world, and each African nonlandlocked country takes the average value of the nonlandlocked countries in the developing world. African importers see a roughly 7 percentage point decline in the iceberg[8] costs of importing, with minor variations across sectors and source regions. African exporters see roughly the same improvement in their iceberg costs of exporting—similarly on an MFN basis. The biggest expected gains from implementation of the TFA are expected in countries such as Cameroon, the Democratic Republic of Congo, Egypt, Nigeria, and Tanzania with a decline in trade costs of 10 percentage points.

**Table 4.2**   Trade facilitation implementation and iceberg trade costs reductions

*percent*

| | Reduction of time in customs due to TFA implementation | Reduction in iceberg trade costs |
|---|---|---|
| Nigeria | 31.8 | 10.0 |
| Congo, Dem. Rep. | 23.7 | 10.0 |
| Cameroon | 17.9 | 10.0 |
| Egypt, Arab Rep. | 16.7 | 10.0 |
| Tanzania | 16.6 | 10.0 |
| Zimbabwe | 15.3 | 10.0 |
| Ethiopia | 11.1 | 10.0 |
| Kenya | 10.9 | 10.0 |
| Côte d'Ivoire | 8.5 | 8.5 |
| Uganda | 5.7 | 5.7 |
| Burkina Faso | 4.5 | 4.5 |
| Ghana | 4.3 | 4.3 |
| Zambia | 4.2 | 4.2 |
| Mauritius | 2.6 | 2.6 |
| Botswana | 2.6 | 2.6 |
| Namibia | 2.6 | 2.6 |
| South Africa | 2.6 | 2.6 |
| Madagascar | 2.1 | 2.1 |
| Rwanda | 2.0 | 2.0 |
| Tunisia | 2.0 | 2.0 |
| Morocco | 1.6 | 1.6 |
| Senegal | 0.3 | 0.3 |
| Mozambique | 0.0 | 0.0 |

*Source:* Estimates, World Bank study team.

*Note:* TFA = trade facilitation agreement.

## NOTES

1. Central Africa = Angola, Cameroon, Central African Republic, Chad, Democratic Republic of Congo, Equatorial Guinea, Gabon, Republic of Congo, Rwanda, and São Tomé and Príncipe; East Africa = Burundi, Comoros, Djibouti, Eritrea, Ethiopia, Kenya, Somalia, South Sudan, Sudan, and Uganda; North Africa = Algeria, Arab Republic of Egypt, Libya, Morocco, and Tunisia; southern Africa = Botswana, Eswatini, Lesotho, Madagascar, Malawi, Mauritius, Mozambique, Namibia, the Seychelles, South Africa, Tanzania, Zambia, and Zimbabwe; West Africa = Benin, Burkina Faso, Cabo Verde, Côte d'Ivoire, Ghana, Guinea, Guinea-Bissau, Liberia, Mali, Mauritania, Niger, Nigeria, Senegal, Sierra Leone, The Gambia, and Togo.

2. Among others, in the context of the Belt and Road Initiative (Maliszewska and van der Mensbrugghe 2019) and the Comprehensive and Progressive Trans-Pacific Partnership (Maliszewska, Olekseyuk, and Osorio-Rodarte 2018).

3. The origin of dynamic microsimulation can be traced back to the 1950s seminal work of Orcutt (1957), whose contributions sought to overcome the limitations of models available at that time. Orcutt observed that the earlier models could be used to predict the aggregate impact, but they could not describe the distributional impact of policy reforms or the effects on inequality of long-term trends such as demographic change. Data availability and modeling have advanced significantly since then, and yet dynamic microsimulations remain the main tool for studying distributional change and providing the unique perspective of projecting samples of population forward in time.

4. Female labor intensity for each country is measured as the share of female employment in an economic activity divided by the share of female employment in the country. In the formula for female labor intensity $(FLI_a)$, $f_a$ and $m_a$ are the female and male labor volumes in activity $a$, respectively:

$$FLI_a = \frac{\dfrac{f_a}{f_a + m_a}}{\dfrac{\Sigma_a f_a}{\Sigma_a (f_a + m_a)}}; \forall_a \{activities\}.$$

5. Future work will carefully assess the content of the AfCFTA agreement relative to the existing subregional African regional trade agreements (RTAs) to quantify the exact reduction in trade costs associated with NTBs.

6. The nature of the NTBs would decide the extent to which they can be changed bilaterally. These scenarios take the maximal position—that is, the measures are affected no matter the source of the imports.

7. Row L is a weighted average of the following components: (1) information availability; (2) involvement of the trade community; (3) advance rulings; (4) appeal procedures; (5) fees and charges; (6) formalities involving documents; (7) formalities involving automation; (8) formalities involving procedures; (9) internal border agency cooperation; (10) external border agency cooperation; and (11) governance and impartiality.

8. The assumption of iceberg trade costs implies that a fraction of the good is lost in transport due to transport costs as originally proposed by Samuelson (1954).

## REFERENCES

Aboudou, F., A. Oga, M. Tassou, and K. Alamou. 2017. "Study on the Specific Problems of Women Traders in the Abidjan-Lagos Corridor." Report prepared for Laboratoire d'Analyse Régionale et d'Expertise Sociale (LARES) for Borderless Alliance.

Aggarwal, Aradhna, Mombert Hoppe, and Peter Walkenhorst. 2019. *Special Economic Zones in South Asia: Industrial Islands or Vehicles for Diversification?* Washington, DC: World Bank Group.

Aguiar, Angel, Maksym Chepeliev, Erwin L. Corong, Robert McDougall, and Dominique van der Mensbrugghe. 2019. "The GTAP Data Base: Version 10." *Journal of Global Economic Analysis* 4 (1): 1–27. https://doi.org/10.21642/jgea.040101af.

Bourguignon, François, and Maurizio Bussolo. 2013. "Income Distribution in Computable General Equilibrium Modeling." In *Handbook of Computable General Equilibrium Modeling*, 1: 1383–437. Amsterdam: Elsevier.

Bourguignon, François, Maurizio Bussolo, and Luiz Awazu Pereira da Silva. 2008. *The Impact of Macroeconomic Policies on Poverty and Income Distribution: Macro-Micro Evaluation Techniques and Tools.* Washington, DC: World Bank.

Brenton, Paul, Elisa Gamberoni, and Catherine Sear. 2013. *Women and Trade in Africa: Realizing the Potential.* Washington, DC: World Bank.

Brenton, Paul, and Carmine Soprano. 2018. "Small-Scale Cross-Border Trade in Africa: Why It Matters and How It Should Be Supported." Bridges Africa 7. https://www.ictsd.org/bridges-news /bridges-africa/news/small-scale-cross-border-trade-in-africa-why-it-matters-and-how-it.

Bussolo, Maurizio, Rafael E. De Hoyos, and Denis Medvedev. 2010. "Economic Growth and Income Distribution: Linking Macro-Economic Models with Household Survey Data at the Global Level." *International Journal of Microsimulation* 3 (1): 92–103.

de Melo, J., and Z. Sorgho. 2019. "The Landscape of Rules of Origin across African RECs in a Comparative Perspectives with Suggestions for Harmonization." Fondation pour Les Études et Recherches sur le Développement International, Clermont-Ferrand, France.

Golub, Stephen. 2015. "Informal Cross-Border Trade and Smuggling in Africa." In *Handbook on Trade and Development,* edited by Olivier Morrissey, Richardo Lopez, and Kishor Sharma. Cheltenham Glos, U.K.: Edward Elgar Publishing. https://doi.org/10.4337/9781781005316.00016.

Hummels, David, and Georg Schaur. 2012. "Time as a Trade Barrier." NBER working paper, National Bureau of Economic Research, Cambridge, MA.

Jafari, Yaghoob, and David G. Tarr. 2015. "Estimates of Ad Valorem Equivalents of Barriers against Foreign Suppliers of Services in Eleven Services Sectors and 103 Countries." *World Economy* 40 (3): 544–73. https://doi.org/10.1111/twec.12329.

Kee, Hiau Looi, Alessandro Nicita, and Marcelo Olarreaga. 2009. "Estimating Trade Restrictiveness Indices." *Economic Journal.* https://doi.org/10.1111/j.1468-0297.2008.02209.x.

Maliszewska, Maryla, and Dominique van der Mensbrugghe. 2019. "The Belt and Road Initiative Economic, Poverty and Environmental Impacts." Working Paper 8814, World Bank, Washington, DC.

Maliszewska, Maryla, Zoryana Olekseyuk, and Israel Osorio-Rodarte. 2018. "Economic and Distributional Impacts of Comprehensive and Progressive Agreement for Trans-Pacific Partnership: The Case of Vietnam." Working Paper 124022, World Bank, Washington, DC.

Mitaritonna, Cristina, Sami Bensassi, and Joachim Jarreau. 2018. "Regional Integration and Informal Trade in Africa: Evidence from Benin's Borders." *Journal of African Economies* 28 (2): 89–118.

Orcutt, Guy H. 1957. "A New Type of Socio-Economic System." *Review of Economics and Statistics* 39 (2): 116. https://doi.org/10.2307/1928528.

Petri, Peter A., and Michael G. Plummer. 2016. "The Economic Effects of the Trans-Pacific Partnership: New Estimates." Working Paper 16-2, Peterson Institute for International Economics, Washington, DC. https://doi.org/10.2139/ssrn.2723413.

Samuelson, Paul. 1954. "The Transfer Problem and Transport Costs, II: Analysis of Effects of Trade Impediments." *Economic Journal* 64 (254): 264–89. doi:10.2307/2226834.JSTOR 2226834.

UN DESA (United Nations Department of Economic and Social Affairs). 2019. *World Population Prospects 2019.* New York: United Nations.

van der Mensbrugghe, Dominique. 2013. "LINKAGE Technical Reference Document Version 7.1." http://siteresources.worldbank.org/INTPROSPECTS/Resources/334934-1314986341738/TechRef7.1 _01Mar2011.pdf.

WCO (World Customs Organization). 2015. "Developing Policies with Respect to Informal Trade." Brussels, Belgium.

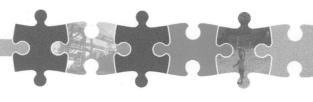

# 5 Macroeconomic Impacts of AfCFTA

The African Continental Free Trade Area (AfCFTA) benefits member countries by lowering costs for consumers and producers, reducing administrative red tape, and reducing compliance costs. The reduction in tariffs will lower the prices of imported goods for consumers, as well as for producers using intermediate inputs. Nontariff barriers (NTBs) take the form of burdensome administrative procedures and various technical requirements. Sanitary and phytosanitary standards or technical standards are in place to protect consumer welfare and safety, but differences in regulations and standards across countries lead to compliance costs, and they are sometimes used as barriers to trade. The deep commitments under AfCFTA are expected to reduce these costs. Similar to tariffs, the reductions in NTBs benefit consumers of final (household) and intermediate goods (firms).

Reductions in trade costs brought about by trade facilitation measures are captured as iceberg trade costs. With the implementation of trade facilitation reforms, such as improving border infrastructure and reducing the cost of administrative procedures, the price of exports and imports declines and transporting a unit of exports or imports requires fewer trade and transportation services. Overall, with lower trade costs, the price of a unit of imports is less expensive, thereby increasing the competitiveness of local production (using imported inputs) either sold on the domestic market or exported. As a result, production shifts to the most competitive sectors, leading to productivity gains and expansion of trade and faster economic growth in the AfCFTA region. The trade cost reductions also apply to trade with non-AfCFTA countries, leading to somewhat faster growth in trade with those countries as well.

Better market access to regional markets allows countries to benefit from faster growth of exports, whereas reduction of a country's own barriers coupled with a reduction of barriers in regional markets leads to lower prices of imports. The differences in gains across countries are linked to the initial level of tariffs, NTBs, and border costs and their reductions under AfCFTA, as well as to the initial level of intra-Africa trade. The overall welfare implications are also linked to the sectors of comparative advantage. If sectors benefiting under AfCFTA have higher productivity than those that would be expanding in the baseline scenario, the reallocation of production leads to faster econo-mywide productivity gains and income growth.

The results of this study assume full implementation of AfCFTA and should be interpreted with caution. Appendix I describes how to maximize the potential benefits of AfCFTA. On the one hand, partial reforms would lead to smaller macroeconomic effects. On the other hand, the framework does not capture the dynamic gains from trade. It is expected that AfCFTA members will enjoy faster productivity gains by tak-ing advantage of the economies of scale in the larger market, as well as attract foreign direct investment. This report returns to this issue in chapter 8. This study abstracts from the impact of COVID-19 on the world economy. Box 5.1 analyzes how the pandemic and the policies to contain it will affect economic activity in Sub-Saharan Africa.

## Box 5.1    The impact of COVID-19 on economic activity in Sub-Saharan Africa

The COVID-19 pandemic has taken a toll on human life and brought major disruption to economic activity across the world. The impact of this unprecedented crisis on human life and the global econ-omy reflects the speed and magnitude of the contagion; greater global integration; and the major role that China plays in global supply chains, travel, and commodity markets. Despite its late arrival, the COVID-19 virus has spread rapidly across Sub-Saharan Africa. The insufficient testing capacity in many countries in the region suggests that the number of cases in some countries most likely understate the true number of infections.

Economic growth in Sub-Saharan Africa is projected to decline from 2.4 percent in 2019 to between −2.1 to −5.1 percent in 2020, the first recession in the region in the past quarter century. It will cost the region between US\$37 billion and US\$79 billion in terms of output losses for 2020. The downward growth revision in 2020 reflects macroeconomic risks arising from the sharp decline in output growth among the region's key trading partners, including China and the Euro area, the fall in commodity prices, and reduced tourism activity in several countries, as well as the effects of measures to contain the COVID-19 global pandemic.

The impact of COVID-19 on economic activity is conducted under a baseline and downside scenario. The difference between them is that the duration of the pandemic is shorter and the policy response is effective in the baseline, while the pandemic lingers into 2021 and the policy response is not as effective in the downside scenario. The immediate impact of COVID-19 on growth in Sub-Saharan African economies is substantial in both the baseline and downside scenarios. In the baseline scenario, GDP would be lower than in the reference scenario (that is, the no-COVID-19 scenario) by about 5.7 percent in 2020 and 1 percent in 2021. On this basis, growth in the region would decline from 2.4 percent in 2019 to −2.5 percent in 2020 due to COVID-19. In the downside scenario, the decline in the level of economic activity of the region would be more dramatic; that is, 7.6 percent lower than in the no-COVID scenario in 2020 and 9.8 percent in 2021. Growth in the region would decline from 2.4 percent in 2019 to −5.1 percent in 2020 because of COVID-19.

The adverse impact of the pandemic on household welfare would be equally dramatic. In the baseline scenario, welfare losses amount to 7 percent relative to the no-COVID-19 scenario in 2020. The welfare loss would be greater in the event of a lengthy crisis; that is, 10 percent lower than in the no-COVID-19 scenario in 2020 under the downside scenario. Terms of trade deterioration, as a result of plunging commodity prices, coupled with higher unemployment result in a pronounced welfare loss for households.

*continued*

**Box 5.1    The impact of COVID-19 on economic activity in Sub-Saharan Africa (*continued*)**

The COVID-19 pandemic would affect nearly every sector of the economy, including agriculture and nontradable services, where most of the poorest workers in the region are employed. The extractives sector (oil and mining) experiences the largest decline in production. In the baseline scenario, the level of production of this sector would be about 21.5 percent lower than in the no-COVID-19 scenario in 2020. Services and agricultural production also shrink considerably. In the baseline scenario, the value added of the services sector would be 6.5 percent lower than in the no-COVID-19 scenario in 2020. Agricultural production would be 2.6 percent lower during the same period. The downfall in these sectors indicates that the crisis would severely hit the poorest and the most vulnerable; in particular, it would greatly affect women, who depend heavily on these activities in the region.

The COVID-19 crisis is also contributing to increased food insecurity as currencies are weakening and prices of staple foods are rising in many parts of the region. This is compounded by the rise in export restrictions in some countries (Espitia et al. 2020) and other existing crises in many countries, including the desert locust emergency, drought, climate change, fragility, conflict, violence, and underdeveloped food markets. Although global food stocks are plentiful and many commodity prices are stable, the prices of other staples (such as wheat and rice) are rising when many countries' currencies are weakening. These two factors lead to spikes in consumer prices and contribute to increased food insecurity, particularly for food importers. Household incomes are also falling, reducing demand and contributing to food insecurity for the near poor, poor, and vulnerable, such as refugees and internally displaced persons.

The COVID-19 crisis has the potential to create a severe food security crisis in Africa. Agricultural production is likely to contract between 2.6 percent in the baseline scenario and 7 percent in the downside scenario with trade blockages. Food imports also decline substantially (from 13 percent to 25 percent) due to a combination of higher transaction costs and reduced domestic demand.

Policy responses that result in subregional trade blockages will increase transaction costs and lead to even larger welfare losses. In this region that is dependent on agricultural products, these policies will disproportionately impact household welfare as a result of price increases and supply shortages. Welfare losses would amount to 14 percent relative to the no-COVID scenario if countries were to close their borders to trade. Border closings would disproportionally affect the poor, particularly agricultural workers and unskilled workers in the informal sector. In this context, countries in Sub-Saharan Africa need to take this opportunity to strengthen regional value chains in the context of the African Continental Free Trade Area.

*Sources:* Espitia, Rocha, and Ruta 2020; World Bank 2020.

## REAL INCOME IMPLICATIONS

The real income (equivalent variation[1]) gains from tariff liberalization alone are small at the continental level at 0.22 percent. However, selected countries including Morocco, Namibia, and Senegal, benefit substantially from improved market access in other AfCFTA markets and see their welfare increase more than 1 percent. The relatively small gains associated with tariff liberalization are explained by the high nontariff barriers and trade facilitation bottlenecks that constrain trade in Africa. Removing only one constraint is a necessary but not sufficient condition for real income gains to materialize. Indeed, the gains from tariff liberalization and reduction in NTBs (with the increase in market access to non-African markets) would lead to a gain of 2.4 percent in 2035 for the continent. However, several countries such as Côte d'Ivoire, Morocco, Namibia, and Senegal would see their real income increase by over 5 percent. Under full implementation of the AfCFTA scenario, the continental welfare increases by an additional 4.6 percentage points, implying that substantial gains are to be had from trade facilitation.[2]

Under the AfCFTA scenario, real income would increase by 7 percent by 2035 relative to the baseline for the Africa region—a sizable gain.[3] In monetary terms, the gains represent around US$445 billion in 2035 (at 2014 prices and exchange rates). Although the continent is by far the largest gainer in aggregate, the rest of the world sees an increase of US$76 billion by 2035, which translates into a gain of 0.1 percent relative to the baseline scenario.

The gains are unevenly distributed across the Africa region (figure 5.1 and table 5.1). At the very high end are Côte d'Ivoire with gains of 13 percent, and Zimbabwe with gains of 12 percent, followed by Kenya, Namibia, Democratic Republic of Congo and Tanzania at more than 10 percent. At the lower end are a few countries clustered around a gain of 2 percent, including Madagascar, Malawi, and Mozambique. The gains are very closely related to the initial level of trade barriers and trade costs. Countries

**Figure 5.1**    Equivalent variation, percentage relative to baseline, 2035

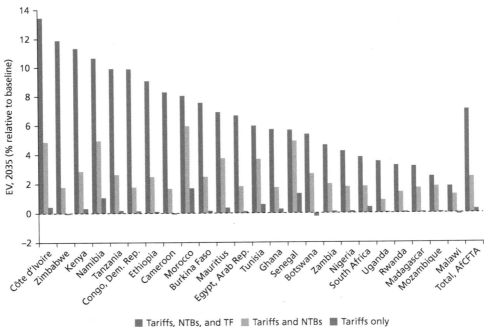

*Source:* Estimates, World Bank study team.

*Note:* Equivalent variation (EV) is the expenditure to attain utility in year *t* in any given simulation using base year prices. AfCFTA = African Continental Free Trade Area; NTB = nontariff barrier; TF = trade facilitation.

**Table 5.1** Percentage deviations from baseline of equivalent variation, exports, and imports, 2035

*percent*

| | EV | | | Exports | | | Imports | | |
|---|---|---|---|---|---|---|---|---|---|
| | Tariffs, NTBs, and TF | Tariffs and NTBs | Tariffs only | Tariffs, NTBs, and TF | Tariffs and NTBs | Tariffs only | Tariffs, NTBs, and TF | Tariffs and NTBs | Tariffs only |
| Côte d'Ivoire | 13.5 | 4.9 | 0.4 | 40.4 | 23.5 | 1.6 | 68.9 | 30.3 | 2.3 |
| Zimbabwe | 12.0 | 1.7 | −0.1 | 47.4 | 25.0 | 0.0 | 57.3 | 19.6 | −0.2 |
| Kenya | 11.4 | 2.8 | 0.3 | 36.0 | 23.7 | 0.8 | 49.4 | 19.2 | 1.0 |
| Namibia | 10.7 | 5.0 | 1.0 | 33.3 | 28.5 | 1.2 | 31.3 | 21.9 | 1.6 |
| Congo, Dem. Rep. | 9.9 | 1.7 | 0.1 | 21.0 | 12.2 | 1.8 | 71.7 | 30.2 | 4.3 |
| Tanzania | 9.9 | 2.6 | 0.2 | 32.4 | 21.1 | 0.4 | 52.1 | 19.8 | 0.6 |
| Ethiopia | 9.0 | 2.4 | 0.1 | 30.6 | 17.4 | 3.6 | 48.4 | 17.2 | 4.1 |
| Cameroon | 8.3 | 1.6 | −0.1 | 45.9 | 23.0 | 7.2 | 61.5 | 22.2 | 7.4 |
| Morocco | 8.1 | 6.0 | 1.7 | 32.6 | 28.0 | 3.1 | 37.0 | 29.2 | 4.6 |
| Burkina Faso | 7.5 | 2.5 | 0.1 | 13.9 | 7.9 | 1.6 | 29.2 | 10.8 | 1.7 |
| Mauritius | 6.9 | 3.8 | 0.3 | 32.9 | 27.0 | 0.7 | 31.7 | 22.5 | 0.8 |
| Egypt, Arab Rep. | 6.7 | 1.8 | 0.1 | 51.5 | 30.1 | 3.1 | 56.2 | 24.0 | 3.1 |
| Tunisia | 5.9 | 3.7 | 0.6 | 31.1 | 27.4 | 1.7 | 33.8 | 25.9 | 2.4 |
| Ghana | 5.7 | 1.7 | 0.2 | 18.7 | 14.3 | 1.1 | 25.6 | 13.3 | 1.1 |
| Senegal | 5.5 | 4.9 | 1.3 | 31.7 | 30.2 | 4.0 | 29.8 | 26.8 | 4.6 |
| Botswana | 5.4 | 2.6 | −0.3 | 13.5 | 10.6 | −0.1 | 18.9 | 12.2 | −0.5 |
| Zambia | 4.7 | 2.0 | 0.1 | 7.9 | 5.6 | 0.1 | 19.6 | 9.9 | 0.3 |
| Nigeria | 4.2 | 1.7 | 0.0 | 26.0 | 15.2 | 1.0 | 44.9 | 19.0 | 1.1 |
| South Africa | 3.8 | 1.8 | 0.4 | 17.6 | 12.5 | 1.4 | 24.7 | 14.9 | 2.0 |
| Uganda | 3.5 | 0.8 | 0.0 | 10.4 | 4.6 | 0.8 | 24.5 | 6.6 | 0.8 |
| Rwanda | 3.2 | 1.0 | 0.0 | 9.3 | 6.4 | 0.4 | 14.2 | 6.3 | 0.3 |
| Madagascar | 3.1 | 1.7 | 0.0 | 19.2 | 13.4 | 2.0 | 23.6 | 14.3 | 2.2 |
| Mozambique | 2.5 | 1.8 | 0.0 | 17.1 | 16.6 | −0.2 | 15.9 | 14.2 | −0.2 |
| Malawi | 1.8 | 1.2 | −0.1 | 12.5 | 12.1 | 1.1 | 13.4 | 10.9 | 0.8 |

*Source:* Estimates, World Bank study team.

*Note:* Equivalent variation (EV) is the expenditure to attain utility in year *t* in any given simulation using base year prices. NTB = nontariff barrier; TF = trade facilitation.

that are already relatively open tend to benefit less from their own liberalization, but they tend to benefit more from improved market access in other markets. Countries that are heavily protected may see a larger reallocation of output across sectors because of heightened import competition, but they are also likely to benefit more from lower imported input prices.

## TRADE IMPLICATIONS

Within the continent, trade will grow substantially (see tables 5.2, 5.3, and 5.4). The volume of total exports increases by almost 29 percent by 2035 (relative to the baseline). Intracontinental exports increase by over 81 percent, while exports to non-African countries increase by 19 percent. Despite these changes, intracontinental trade would remain around 20 percent of total trade for the continent in 2035. Cameroon, the Arab Republic of Egypt, Ghana, Morocco, and Tunisia are expected to benefit from the fastest growth of intra-AfCFTA exports to AfCFTA partners, with exports doubling or tripling with respect to the baseline. The smallest export expansions are expected in Democratic Republic of Congo, Mozambique, and Zambia (10–30 percent). In monetary terms, intracontinental trade grows from US$294 billion in 2035 in the baseline scenario to US$532 billion after implementation of AfCFTA in 2035. By 2035 under AfCFTA, the biggest increase in the value of exports to the regional partners is expected to benefit, in descending order of value, Egypt, Morocco, South Africa, Nigeria, Kenya, and Côte d'Ivoire (between US$48 million and US$11 billion). Similarly, for the welfare gains, the smallest export expansions are expected in the economies that are already relatively open such as Madagascar, Malawi, Mauritius, and Rwanda, with export increases of less than US$1 billion.

Under the AfCFTA scenario, manufacturing exports gain the most, 62 percent overall, with intra-Africa trade increasing by 110 percent and exports to the rest of the world by 46 percent. There are smaller gains in agriculture, 49 percent and 10 percent for intra- and extra-Africa trade, respectively. The gains in the services trade are relatively slight—some 4 percent overall and 14 percent within Africa. The base year trade shares and volumes are relatively slight in services.

In volume terms, manufacturing exports dominate the export picture for Africa. Of the US$2.5 trillion in exports projected in 2035 for Africa, US$823 billion are in manufactures; US$690 billion in natural resources; US$191 billion in agriculture; and the remaining US$256 billion in services. Of the total growth in exports of US$560 billion, the increase in exports of manufactures represents some US$506 billion—an increase of US$220 billion within Africa and US$286 billion with the rest of the world.

Overall, the destination of African exports rises from 15 percent in 2035 in the baseline to over 21 percent in the AfCFTA scenario (table 5.2). For manufactures, the relevant increase is from 24 percent to almost 32 percent. Exports to AfCFTA members expand with very little trade diversion because the decline in exports to non-AfCFTA

**Table 5.2**  Exports under baseline scenario and AfCFTA

*percent*

| | Share of intra-AfCFTA exports in total exports | | | Intra-AfCFTA exports (% deviation from baseline) | | |
|---|---|---|---|---|---|---|
| | Baseline | | AfCFTA | AfCFTA | Tariff liberalization | Tariffs and NTBs |
| | 2020 | 2035 | 2035 | 2035 | 2035 | 2035 |
| Total, Africa | 12 | 15 | 21 | 81 | 22 | 52 |
| Senegal | 36 | 41 | 50 | 63 | 20 | 58 |
| Kenya | 30 | 35 | 43 | 66 | 6 | 36 |
| Namibia | 33 | 32 | 39 | 59 | 20 | 51 |
| Côte d'Ivoire | 26 | 31 | 37 | 66 | 9 | 36 |
| South Africa | 25 | 30 | 37 | 44 | 15 | 33 |
| Rwanda | 17 | 26 | 33 | 38 | 4 | 19 |
| Zambia | 22 | 26 | 30 | 26 | 6 | 14 |
| Malawi | 21 | 24 | 29 | 34 | 5 | 23 |
| Zimbabwe | 23 | 26 | 28 | 59 | 2 | 29 |
| Uganda | 24 | 23 | 28 | 38 | 4 | 17 |
| Tanzania | 18 | 20 | 27 | 77 | 13 | 46 |
| Mozambique | 33 | 28 | 27 | 14 | 3 | 7 |
| Morocco | 7 | 9 | 26 | 278 | 144 | 245 |
| Botswana | 18 | 21 | 26 | 37 | 1 | 27 |
| Burkina Faso | 15 | 19 | 25 | 53 | 4 | 29 |
| Egypt, Arab Rep. | 8 | 10 | 22 | 237 | 55 | 129 |
| Ethiopia | 20 | 17 | 21 | 59 | 12 | 34 |
| Mauritius | 12 | 17 | 20 | 62 | 18 | 48 |
| Cameroon | 11 | 14 | 19 | 100 | 29 | 55 |
| Tunisia | 11 | 13 | 19 | 91 | 45 | 79 |
| Ghana | 9 | 10 | 16 | 94 | 32 | 64 |
| Nigeria | 8 | 10 | 15 | 83 | 13 | 38 |
| Madagascar | 7 | 9 | 10 | 33 | 9 | 21 |
| Congo, Dem. Rep. | 15 | 8 | 9 | 21 | 5 | 15 |

*Source:* Estimates, World Bank study team.

*Note:* AfCFTA = African Continental Free Trade Area; NTB = nontariff barrier.

**Table 5.3**    Imports under baseline scenario and AfCFTA

*percent*

| | Share of intra-AfCFTA imports in total imports | | | Intra-AfCFTA imports (% deviation from baseline) | | |
|---|---|---|---|---|---|---|
| | Baseline | | AfCFTA | AfCFTA | Tariff liberalization | Tariffs and NTBs |
| | 2020 | 2035 | 2035 | 2035 | 2035 | 2035 |
| Total, Africa | 12 | 18 | 25 | 102 | 22 | 52 |
| Botswana | 71 | 72 | 72 | 19 | −1 | 11 |
| Namibia | 6 | 69 | 71 | 34 | 1 | 22 |
| Zimbabwe | 63 | 67 | 66 | 56 | −1 | 17 |
| Zambia | 59 | 63 | 65 | 25 | 0 | 10 |
| Malawi | 44 | 53 | 58 | 24 | 5 | 15 |
| Congo, Dem. Rep. | 40 | 47 | 57 | 106 | 18 | 50 |
| Uganda | 26 | 38 | 48 | 57 | 5 | 16 |
| Rwanda | 31 | 39 | 46 | 35 | 1 | 11 |
| Ghana | 17 | 28 | 40 | 79 | 8 | 32 |
| Mozambique | 32 | 33 | 36 | 25 | −2 | 15 |
| Cameroon | 14 | 20 | 35 | 188 | 68 | 97 |
| Côte d'Ivoire | 20 | 27 | 32 | 101 | 1 | 42 |
| Senegal | 17 | 2 | 32 | 78 | 27 | 59 |
| Ethiopia | 8 | 12 | 25 | 221 | 84 | 105 |
| Kenya | 14 | 20 | 25 | 89 | 5 | 29 |
| South Africa | 13 | 19 | 20 | 32 | 2 | 16 |
| Madagascar | 8 | 10 | 18 | 131 | 56 | 88 |
| Tunisia | 7 | 11 | 16 | 103 | 22 | 58 |
| Mauritius | 10 | 13 | 15 | 43 | −1 | 21 |
| Egypt, Arab Rep. | 3 | 6 | 14 | 293 | 94 | 188 |
| Morocco | 6 | 9 | 12 | 79 | 7 | 39 |
| Nigeria | 4 | 5 | 9 | 157 | 38 | 75 |
| Burkina Faso | 45 | 59 | 6 | 50 | 7 | 21 |
| Tanzania | 13 | 21 | 2 | 103 | −1 | 32 |

*Source:* Estimates, World Bank study team.

*Note:* AfCFTA = African Continental Free Trade Area; NTB = nontariff barrier.

**Table 5.4** Impacts of AfCFTA on trade of member countries, deviation from baseline, 2035

| | AfCFTA | | | | Non-AfCFTA | | | | World | | | |
|---|---|---|---|---|---|---|---|---|---|---|---|---|
| | Exports | | Imports | | Exports | | Imports | | Exports | | Imports | |
| | % | 2014 US$, billions | % | 2014 US$, billions | % | 2014 US$, billions | % | 2014 US$, billions | % | 2014 US$, billions | % | 2014 US$, billions |
| Agriculture | 49 | 12 | 72 | 19 | 10 | 17 | 62 | 20 | 15 | 29 | 66 | 39 |
| Fossil fuel | 8 | 3 | 8 | 3 | 2 | 13 | 7 | 2 | 2 | 15 | 8 | 5 |
| Processed foods | 91 | 29 | 118 | 40 | 45 | 25 | 44 | 31 | 62 | 55 | 67 | 71 |
| Wood and paper products | 98 | 8 | 125 | 12 | 68 | 8 | 31 | 8 | 80 | 17 | 54 | 20 |
| Textiles and wearing apparel | 195 | 22 | 240 | 29 | 47 | 39 | 43 | 31 | 64 | 62 | 70 | 60 |
| Chemical, rubber, and plastic products | 88 | 36 | 114 | 50 | 99 | 51 | 26 | 40 | 94 | 87 | 45 | 89 |
| Manufactures, NES | 177 | 97 | 213 | 121 | 69 | 67 | 25 | 121 | 108 | 164 | 44 | 242 |
| Energy-intensive manufacturing | 75 | 24 | 99 | 34 | 32 | 94 | 28 | 26 | 36 | 118 | 48 | 60 |
| Petroleum and coal products | 12 | 2 | 12 | 2 | 4 | 1 | 7 | 9 | 7 | 4 | 7 | 11 |
| Construction | 19 | 0 | 42 | 0 | 19 | 1 | 10 | 2 | 19 | 1 | 11 | 3 |
| Trade services | 9 | 0 | 25 | 0 | -8 | -2 | 32 | 11 | -8 | -2 | 32 | 11 |
| Road and rail transport services | 35 | 1 | 55 | 1 | 11 | 5 | 46 | 11 | 12 | 5 | 47 | 12 |
| Water transport services | 25 | 0 | 44 | 0 | 33 | 2 | 17 | 1 | 32 | 2 | 18 | 1 |
| Air transport services | 33 | 1 | 53 | 1 | 29 | 7 | 30 | 8 | 29 | 7 | 31 | 9 |
| Communications services | 11 | 0 | 29 | 0 | -13 | -4 | 42 | 6 | -12 | -4 | 41 | 6 |
| Other financial services | 13 | 0 | 32 | 0 | -5 | 0 | 38 | 5 | -4 | 0 | 38 | 5 |
| Other business services | 22 | 0 | 41 | 1 | 16 | 4 | 39 | 39 | 17 | 4 | 39 | 39 |
| Recreational and other services | 3 | 0 | 18 | 0 | -7 | -2 | 19 | 4 | -7 | -2 | 19 | 5 |
| Public services | 9 | 1 | 17 | 3 | -10 | -4 | 26 | 13 | -5 | -3 | 24 | 16 |
| Insurance and real estate services | 35 | 0 | 56 | 0 | 11 | 1 | 46 | 7 | 12 | 1 | 46 | 7 |
| Minerals, NES | 6 | 1 | 6 | 1 | -2 | -1 | 11 | 1 | -1 | -1 | 8 | 2 |
| Total, agriculture | 49 | 12 | 72 | 19 | 10 | 17 | 62 | 20 | 15 | 29 | 66 | 39 |
| Total, manufacturing | 110 | 220 | 137 | 288 | 46 | 286 | 26 | 267 | 62 | 506 | 44 | 554 |
| Total, natural resources | 8 | 4 | 8 | 4 | 2 | 11 | 8 | 3 | 2 | 15 | 8 | 7 |
| Total, services | 14 | 3 | 26 | 6 | 3 | 7 | 33 | 107 | 4 | 10 | 32 | 113 |
| Total | 81 | 239 | 102 | 317 | 19 | 321 | 27 | 397 | 29 | 560 | 41 | 714 |

*Source:* Estimates, World Bank study team.

*Note:* AfCFTA = African Continental Free Trade Area; NES = not elsewhere specified.

regions is negligible and concentrated in a few services sectors and minerals (figure 5.2). As compared with the baseline, by 2035, exports of minerals to the European Union and China are smaller under AfCFTA.

The biggest expansion of exports to regional partners is recorded in manufactures, not elsewhere specified, followed by energy-intensive manufacturing; chemical, rubber, and plastic products; and processed food products. Among services, the biggest expansion to regional partners is expected in health and education services; air, road, and rail transport services; and other business services. However, the volume of export growth is much smaller than in agriculture and manufacturing. The same sectors would also be expected to expand their exports to non-AfCFTA partners, with significant gains in the exports of several manufacturing sectors and agricultural products.

The volume of total imports is also very substantial, increasing by 41 percent relative to the baseline for 2035 (table 5.4). For intracontinental trade, imports from inside the region expand by 102 percent, and imports from outside the region increase by 25 percent. In value terms, there is an increase in imports of US$310 billion in the baseline scenario, compared with the AfCFTA scenario in which that increase reaches US$627 billion in imports. In terms of share of intracontinental trade, it rises from 18 percent in the baseline to 25 percent with AfCFTA because the share from the rest of the world has a small reduction from 82 percent in the baseline to 75 percent with AfCFTA, which is still very substantial.

**Figure 5.2**   Total exports from Africa, deviation from baseline, 2035

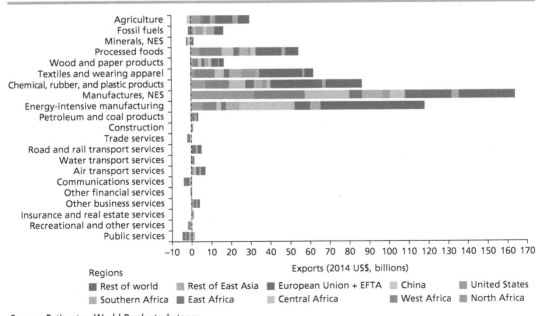

*Source:* Estimates, World Bank study team.

*Note:* EFTA = European Free Trade Association; NES = not elsewhere specified.

For the baseline scenario, intracontinental imports increase from 12 percent in 2020 to 18 percent in 2035 (table 5.3). In the scenario in which AfCFTA is implemented, the increase is to 25 percent in 2035, or 7 percent more than in the baseline scenario. By 2035, and under AfCFTA, the countries that benefit the most from the higher increases of imports are Côte d'Ivoire, the Democratic Republic of Congo, Egypt, Ghana, Kenya, Nigeria, South Africa, and Tanzania, where imports increase within a range of between between US$10 billion and US$32 billion. The smaller expansions in imports are expected in economies such as Malawi, Mauritius, and Rwanda, with import increases of less than US$1 billion.

Under AfCFTA, there is also an expansion of total imports from non-AfCFTA members, with no trade diversion (figure 5.3). The sector showing the highest expansion of imports is manufactures, not elsewhere specified. Among AfCFTA regions, North Africa experiences the highest growth, whereas for non-AfCFTA members, the imports increase mainly from China and the European Union. Three sectors—chemical, rubber, and plastic products; processed foods; and textiles—also see their imports expanding, with North and West Africa having an important role in that expansion. Among services sectors, imports increase fastest in other business services, with the highest increase in imports from the European Union. The expansion of trade in services is muted because of the initial low levels of trade in services.

**Figure 5.3** Total imports from Africa, deviation from baseline, 2035

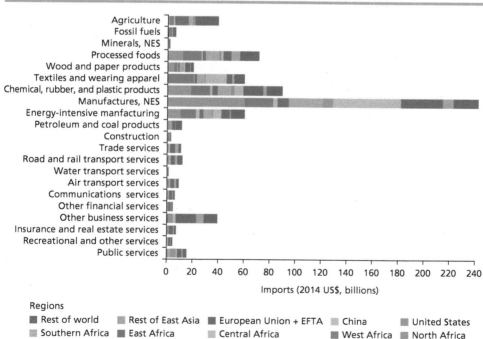

*Source:* Estimates, World Bank study team.

*Note:* EFTA = European Free Trade Association; NES = not elsewhere specified.

## OUTPUT IMPLICATIONS

AfCFTA is expected to boost regional output by US$211 billion by 2035 (figure 5.4). The impacts on output are highly varied across sectors. In broad terms, output rises most in natural resources and services (1.7 percent) and manufacturing (1.2 percent), whereas agriculture declines (0.5 percent) relative to the baseline in 2035. In terms of volume of output, most of the gains will be realized by the services sector (US$147 billion), with smaller gains in manufacturing (US$56 billion) and natural resources (US$17 billion) and a small decline in agriculture (US$8 billion) compared with the baseline in 2035. Relative to the baseline in 2035, agriculture is growing faster in all parts of Africa except in North Africa, which under AfCFTA is shifting toward manufacturing, not elsewhere specified; chemical, rubber, and plastic products; as well as trade services, transport services, and recreation services. East African economies as an aggregate seem to specialize more in agricultural products and services, with productive factors shifting away from the selected manufacturing sectors to take advantage of more profitable opportunities in the growing sectors. Trade in natural resources will grow in Central and West Africa under AfCFTA, whereas it will decline in other regions as compared

**Figure 5.4**   Output difference relative to baseline, 2035

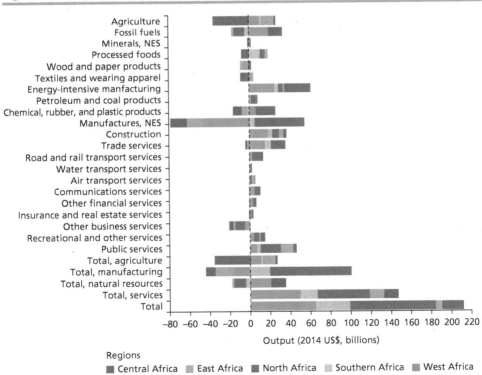

*Source:* Estimates, World Bank study team.

*Note:* NES = not elsewhere specified.

to the baseline. Services will expand across all regions driven by increasing demand as incomes in Africa rise.

The aggregate numbers mask a lot of heterogeneity of outcomes across countries. Of the 24 economies represented in the simulations, the relative importance of agriculture increases in 14 countries, natural resources in 12 countries, manufacturing in 6 countries, and services in 13 countries. Even while manufacturing's share of output falls for the majority of countries, the volume of manufacturing will continue to increase under AfCFTA. In fact, in 15 of the 24 countries, the value of output of manufacturing is higher under AfCFTA in 2035 than under the baseline scenario, and the output of several manufacturing sectors expands, just at a slower pace compared with other sectors. Similarly, for agriculture, the volume of output under AfCFTA by 2035 is higher than under the baseline in 15 out of 24 countries, while for services, the volume is higher under AfCFTA in 21 countries, partially reflecting the positive income elasticity of services.

A number of factors explain the impact on output. In the standard Armington framework, a decline in import prices, which in these simulations vary highly across sectors, leads to higher spending on imports compared with domestic production. In the absence of exports, this leads to an absolute decline in production. Exports nevertheless do increase, driven by real exchange rate depreciation, a reduction in production costs (as a result of the lower cost of imported intermediates), the assumed improvement in trade facilitation for African exporters, and the improvement in market access in Africa and the rest of the world.

The key question is whether the import-driven expenditure switching from domestic consumption is greater than the increase in exports. This will depend on four additional factors:

1. The import exposure of the sector—that is, the level of imports relative to domestic absorption. If the import share is relatively low, the impact on domestic markets will be attenuated.
2. The ease of substitution between imports and domestic goods
3. The export exposure of domestic production
4. The ex ante decrease in the price of imports—that is, the sum of the change in import tariffs, the nontariff barrier ad valorem equivalent (AVE), and the import component of the trade facilitation agreement (TFA).

In a two-sector economy, the sector with the highest decline in import tariffs would see a relatively larger impact on domestic production—that is, there would be more expenditure switching. Resources would then flow to the sector that is subject to the smallest decline in import prices. On average, agriculture and manufacturing see an ex ante import price decline of 28 percent and 24 percent, respectively, and services only 16 percent (and even less for natural resources). This finding implies that, all else being equal, one would expect to see a reallocation of production toward services and away from agriculture and manufacturing, which is observed in broad terms.

There are significant variations across sectors. For example, in agriculture, the import exposure overall is relatively low (only 6 percent) and the import price shock is 28 percent. At the same time, the domestic output is mostly oriented toward the domestic market. In this situation, expenditure switching is a more important factor than export expansion and resources flow to other sectors. The energy-intensive sector is an interesting counterexample. The import intensity is high at nearly 40 percent, and the import price shock is also relatively high at 27 percent, and yet output expands substantially—some 9.5 percent. However, exports in the baseline already account for a high percentage of domestic output, and thus export expansion is a more important factor than domestic expenditure switching. Manufacturing, not elsewhere specified, is another sector in which output declines. It is also highly exposed—some 50 percent—but with a relatively low export base. Among services, other business services are the only services to see a decline in output. But they are one of the most exposed services, with an import share of 22 percent in the baseline, and also one that receives the largest import price shock (some 28 percent). Thus expenditure switching plays a large role in this service sector.

## GOVERNMENT REVENUE IMPLICATIONS

AfCFTA's short-term impact on tax revenues is small for most countries.[4] Tariff revenues would decline by less than 1.5 percent for most countries except for the Democratic Republic of Congo (3.4 percent), The Gambia (2.7 percent), the Republic of Congo (2.1 percent), and Zambia (1.6 percent). Total tax revenues would seldom decline by more than 0.3 percent, except for Djibouti (0.5 percent), the Republic of Congo (0.6 percent), The Gambia (0.9 percent), and the Democratic Republic of Congo (0.9 percent). Two factors help explain these small revenue impacts. First, imports from African countries account for a small share of tariff revenues for most countries (less than 10 percent on average). Second, most tariff revenues can be shielded from liberalization with exclusion lists because these revenues are highly concentrated in a few tariff lines (1 percent of tariff lines account for more than three-quarters of intra-Africa tariff revenues in almost all African countries). These results are consistent with other studies that show that, even under full liberalization, the number of countries that will experience significant tariff revenue losses is small, and exclusion lists have the potential to significantly reduce such losses (ADB 2019; Laborde et al. 2019; UNECA 2017).

In the medium term, the overall impact on import tariff revenue is expected to be positive in the AfCFTA scenario at the regional level. Although tariffs decline, the increase in the volume of imports leads to higher tariff revenue collection, with an increase of 3 percent at the continental level compared with the baseline in 2035. Faster economic growth leading to a higher level of economic activity is likely to increase the total revenue from other taxes as well.

In the scenario in which only tariffs are reduced, the fiscal revenue from import taxes declines by almost 10 percent at the continental level. Again, aggregate results mask large heterogeneity in impacts across countries. In fact, in the simulations, 10 out of 24 countries may see a decline of tax revenues from imports in the AfCFTA scenario compared with the baseline in 2035, including Burkina Faso, Cameroon, the Democratic Republic of Congo, Ethiopia, Ghana, Madagascar, Malawi, Rwanda, Uganda, and Zambia. Overall government revenues are very difficult to predict, however, because the model used in this study is not best suited to follow other taxes when analyzing scenarios up to 2035, and so these results should be treated with caution, and further research is needed in this area.

## NOTES

1. Equivalent variation is the expenditure to attain utility in year $t$ in any given simulation using base year prices.

2. The TFA simulations do not include specific measures to improve trade facilitation. Some measures may have a relatively low cost, but others may require investments in software, other logistical support, and infrastructure, among other things. These costs could reduce the net gains from improvements in trade facilitation, depending in part on the source of financing.

3. Real income is measured by equivalent variation. It is similar in magnitude to real private consumption.

4. Arenas and Vnukova (2019) estimate the short-term impacts of AfCFTA's tariff liberalization on imports and tax revenues using a partial equilibrium model (see appendix J).

## REFERENCES

ADB (African Development Bank). 2019. *African Economic Outlook 2019.* Abidjan, Côte d'Ivoire: ADB.

Arenas, Guillermo, and Yulia Vnukova. 2019. "Short-Term Revenue Implications of Tariff Liberalization under the African Continental Free Trade Area (AfCFTA)." World Bank, Washington, DC.

Espitia, Alvaro, Nadia Rocha, and Michele Ruta. 2020. "Covid-19 and Food Protectionism: The Impact of the Pandemic and Export Restrictions on World Food Markets." Policy Research Working Paper No. WPS 9253. World Bank, Washington, DC.

Laborde, David, Tess Lallemant, Kieran Mcdougal, and Carin Smaller. 2019. "Transforming Agriculture in Africa and Asia: What Are the Policy Priorities?" Policy brief, International Institute for Sustainable Development, Winnipeg, Canada.

UNECA (United Nations Economic Commission for Africa). 2017. "Assessing Regional Integration in Africa VIII: Bringing the Continental Free Trade Area About." Addis Ababa, Ethiopia.

World Bank. 2020. *Africa's Pulse* 21. World Bank, Washington, DC.

# 6 Distributional Effects of AfCFTA on Poverty and Employment

## EFFECTS ON POVERTY

According to the latest estimate from the World Bank (2018), on the African continent 415 million people live in extreme poverty (57 percent of global total) and 60 percent of people reside in countries with fragile situations.[1] Progress toward reaching development goals, including poverty reduction, is heterogeneous across the continent. On a broad regional level, for example, the level of extreme poverty in North Africa is less than 3 percent, whereas that of Sub-Saharan Africa is 41.1 percent. These regional estimates, however, mask strong discrepancies between countries. In North Africa, the extreme poverty headcount ratio in Djibouti is 19.3 percent, but the same ratio for Algeria and the Arab Republic of Egypt is below 0.4 percent. In Sub-Saharan Africa, incidences of extreme poverty are the lowest in Mauritius (0.4 percent), the Seychelles (0.9 percent), and Gabon (3.9 percent), and the highest in Burundi (74.8 percent), Madagascar (77.5 percent), and the Central African Republic (77.7 percent).

By 2035 and under baseline conditions, the headcount ratio for extreme poverty in Africa is projected to decline to 10.9 percent. Perhaps seeing a continuation of current demographic and economic trends, and in line with poverty projections from the World Bank (2018), the world remains off-target to eradicate extreme poverty by 2030. In the baseline scenario and throughout Africa, the headcount ratio of extreme poverty is expected to decline from 34.7 percent in 2015 to 15.5 percent by 2030 and 10.9 percent by 2035.[2] Throughout this period, Sub-Saharan Africa would observe a decline in extreme poverty to 13.1 percent from the most recent estimate of 41.1 percent. Most countries in North Africa[3] would be expected to eradicate extreme poverty by 2035.

More than half of Africa's population is likely to live on more than US$5.50, adjusted for purchasing power parity (PPP), a day by 2035. Under baseline projections, the proportion of people who live above moderate poverty, here defined above an international threshold of PPP US$5.50 a day,[4] is expected to increase in Africa from 21.9 percent in 2015 to more than half of the population by 2035,[5] which is equivalent to a net increase of half a billion people. In this analysis's baseline projections, this expansion is reflected in a higher demand for basic public services such as education, health, electricity, and water.

Full implementation of the African Continental Free Trade Area (AfCFTA) could by 2035 lift an additional 30 million people, or 1.5 percent of the continent's population, out of extreme poverty (see figure 6.1, panel a). West Africa would observe a decline of 12 million attributable to AfCFTA, while Central and East Africa would observe declines of 9.3 million and 4.8 million, respectively. At the country level, the largest gains in poverty reduction from implementation of AfCFTA would occur in countries with high initial poverty rates such as Guinea-Bissau (10.2 percentage points), Mali (7.6), Sierra Leone (7.2), Togo (7.2), Liberia (5.7), Niger (5.4), and the Central African Republic (5.1).

Meanwhile, full implementation of the agreement could lift 67.9 million in the continent out of moderate poverty (at US$5.50, PPP-adjusted, a day) by 2035 (see figure 6.1, panel b), and in part because of the influence of the large boost in household consumption expected from trade openness, about half of the people lifted from moderate poverty would be located in six countries: Ethiopia (8.2 million), Nigeria (7 million), Tanzania (6.3 million), the Democratic Republic of Congo (4.8 million), Kenya (4.4 million), and Niger (4.2 million).

**Figure 6.1**   Evolution of extreme and moderate poverty under baseline and AfCFTA implementation, 2015–35

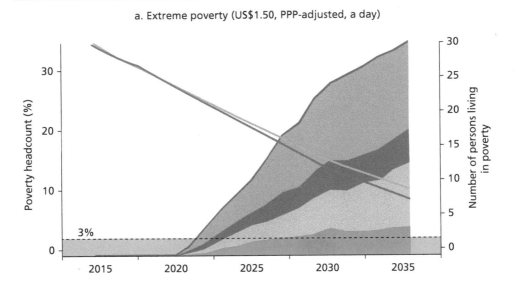

a. Extreme poverty (US$1.50, PPP-adjusted, a day)

*continued*

**Figure 6.1**  Evolution of extreme and moderate poverty under baseline and AfCFTA implementation, 2015–35 *(continued)*

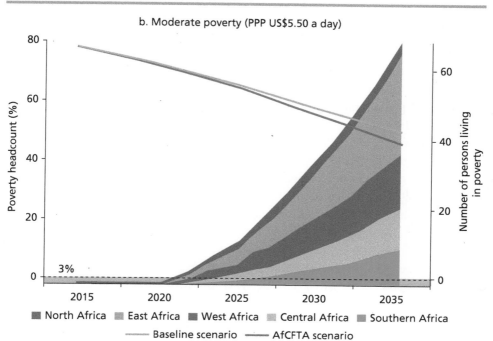

b. Moderate poverty (PPP US$5.50 a day)

North Africa ■ East Africa ■ West Africa ■ Central Africa ■ Southern Africa
——— Baseline scenario ——— AfCFTA scenario

*Source:* Estimates, World Bank study team.

*Note:* The dashed line indicates the World Bank target for reducing the global poverty headcount ratio to 3 percent by 2030. For moderate poverty, the 3 percent target is only indicative. See figure 0.2 in the Overview for a definition of the regions. AfCFTA = African Continental Free Trade Area; PPP = purchasing power parity.

## EFFECTS ON EMPLOYMENT

This analysis focuses on workers switching jobs. In standard computable general equilibrium (CGE) models, unemployment is fixed at the benchmark level. The number of jobs grows only in line with the growth of the working-age population over time and remains exogenous under different scenarios (this assumption is relaxed in the sensitivity analysis).[6] Thus the analysis does not capture the effects of AfCFTA on job creation, but rather its impacts on job reallocation as employment shifts from sectors of comparative disadvantage to sectors of comparative advantage. This analysis therefore focuses on workers switching jobs or on labor displacement, not job creation. Under baseline conditions and at the continental level, the distribution of employment by activity changes according to expected demographic and urbanization trends.

Under baseline conditions, agriculture and wholesale and retail trade would provide half of employment in the continent. Agriculture's importance as a source of employment is expected to decline in 2035 to 29.7 percent of total employment in Africa, down from 35.9 percent in 2020. This decline is in line with historical trends globally and for the African continent. The wholesale and retail trade sector's participation in total employment is expected to increase from 16.9 percent in 2020 to 20 percent by 2035.

Agriculture would, under baseline conditions, account for one-quarter of employment in the continent, with marked differences between countries. In North Africa, the percentage of people employed in agriculture would be lower than in other regions, at 10.7 percent. In Egypt, agriculture is expected to employ 12.4 percent of the workforce by 2035, and in Morocco, 11.6 percent, but smaller proportions are projected for Tunisia (7.8 percent) and the rest of North Africa (6.1 percent). For East Africa, the proportion of employment in agriculture is projected to be 47.8 percent, driven by the large shares in Kenya (60.9 percent), Ethiopia (60.7 percent), and Uganda (52.1 percent), compared with lower shares in the countries that make up the rest of East Africa (with 11.4 percent of employment in agriculture by 2035). In southern Africa, with an employment projection in agriculture of 29.8 percent, the largest agriculture employment share is projected for Madagascar (53.1 percent) and Tanzania (50.4 percent), and the lowest for Botswana (4.9 percent) and South Africa (1.7 percent). Meanwhile, West Africa's agricultural employment is projected to be 26.7 percent by 2035, while that of the Central Africa region will be 20.9 percent, with more homogeneous conditions between countries.

Under baseline conditions, the wholesale and retail trade sector would be the second most important employer in the continent. Across the continent, the wholesale and retail trade sector is expected to reach 21.1 percent of employment, but this proportion is expected to be larger in some countries such as Nigeria (with a 41 percent employment share for trade employment). In North, East, Central, and southern Africa, the trade employment share is on average 18 percent.

After trade, the most important sectors for employment are related to public services (education, health, electricity, water, and public administration), with 15.2 percent in the continent, followed by other business services (3.2 percent), recreational services (2.5 percent), and communications services (2.2 percent).

AfCFTA would support the structural transformation of employment in Africa. Figure 6.2 shows that, as a result of the agreement, the continent would see a net increase in the volume of workers in energy-intensive manufacturing (such as steel and aluminum with an increase of 2.4 million), public services (4.6 million), recreational and other services (0.28 million), and trade services (0.13 million). A more careful examination of the results at the country level reveals differentiated impacts across countries. For example, agricultural employment as a percentage of total employment is increasing in 15 countries[7] and declining in 14, which reflects the large sectoral redistribution of agricultural output across the continent (figure 6.2).

Sectoral reallocation of labor within countries is driven by the intensity of labor used and the reduction of trade costs under AfCFTA. The effect on segments of the population

**Figure 6.2**   AfCFTA employment change with respect to baseline, total and female

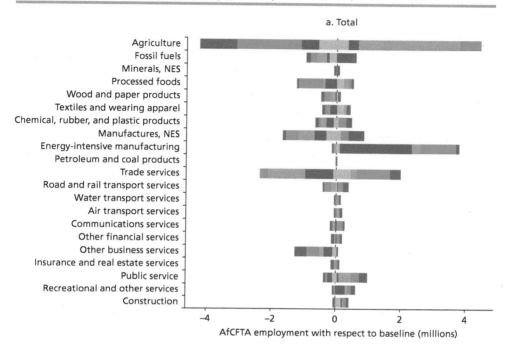

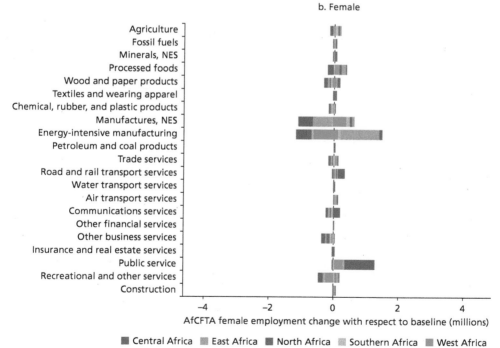

*Source:* Estimates, World Bank study team.

*Note:* AfCFTA = African Continental Free Trade Area; NES = not elsewhere specified.

is driven as well by the propensity of people, particularly women, to be employed in certain industries. Across the African continent, the sector that tends to employ a larger proportion of women is recreational and other services.[8] Although at the continental level, recreational and other services are not affected in terms of total employment, nuanced differences emerge when looking at the regional level. For example, as a result of AfCFTA, Central Africa would observe combined gains of 287,000 jobs in recreational and other services. Again within Central Africa, Cameroon and the Central African Republic would observe gains, while there would be a decline in Rwanda. Figure 6.2, panel b, shows the results for women at the continental level. Major gains in employment are expected in the agriculture sector (0.3 million), which is overall close to gender neutrality in employment across Africa (see figure 4.1 in chapter 4).

In general terms, wages for unskilled labor would grow at a faster rate than average in West, East, and southern Africa. Figures 6.3 and 6.4 summarize the effects of full implementation of AfCFTA on wages at the regional level. Effects on relative wages are driven by the changes in the composition of output induced by the policy reforms. In East, West, and southern Africa, AfCFTA is expected to reduce the skill wage premia because remuneration for unskilled labor would grow at a faster rate than for skilled labor (initial gender and skill premia are reported in table 4.1 in chapter 4). In East Africa, the wages of unskilled labor would grow 0.16 percentage points more (year-on-year) than the wages of skilled workers; in West Africa, 0.03 percentage points; and in southern Africa, the same number of percentage points. Skill premia are expected to increase in North Africa

**Figure 6.3**     Effects of AfCFTA on wages by skill

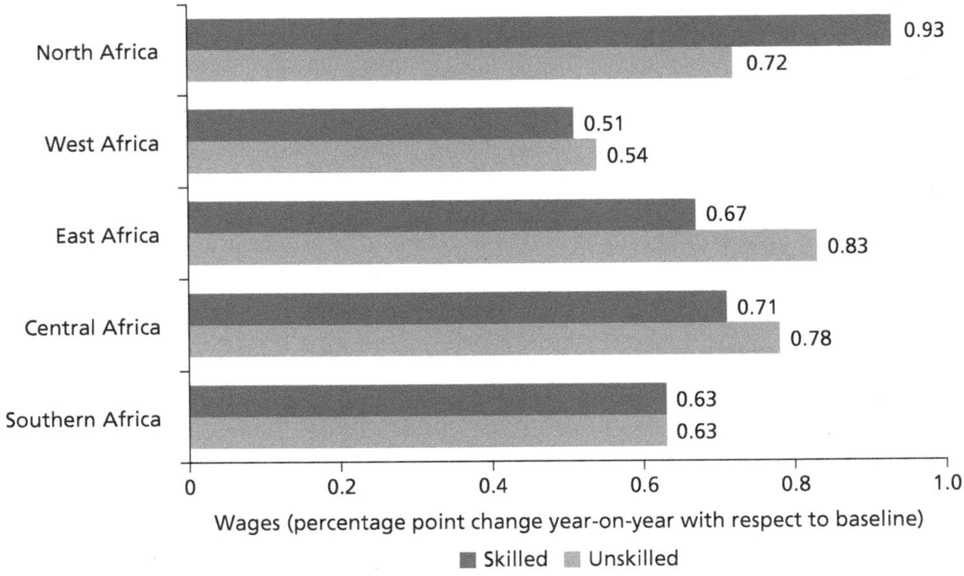

Wages (percentage point change year-on-year with respect to baseline)

■ Skilled ■ Unskilled

*Source:* Estimates, World Bank study team.

*Note:* AfCFTA = African Continental Free Trade Area.

**Figure 6.4**   Effects of AfCFTA on wages by gender

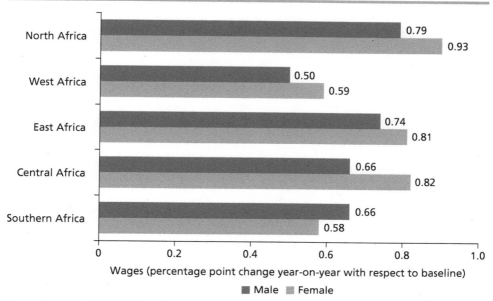

Source: Estimates, World Bank study team.

Note: AfCFTA = African Continental Free Trade Area.

amid the increase in the demand for skilled workers in manufactures and sophisticated services due to AfCFTA. Wages for skilled workers would grow 0.2 percentage points (year-on-year) higher than those of unskilled workers.

As a result of an expansion of output in female labor–intensive industries, female wages would grow faster in all regions except southern Africa. As for baseline conditions, females' wages would grow faster than males' wages in Central Africa (0.17 percentage points), North Africa (0.11 percentage points), West Africa (0.09 percentage points), and East Africa (0.07 percentage points), amid an increase in female employment in agriculture and some key services sectors that tend to employ larger shares of women (see figure 6.2). Wages for female workers would grow at a slower pace than those for males in southern Africa (0.07 percentage points). Although these results take into account that male and female workers are imperfect substitutes, they also assume frictionless mobility of workers between sectors and fixed labor force participation rates. As a result of output expansion in key female labor–intensive industries, females' wages would grow faster than males' wages in 19 countries.[9] Overall, these results are upper-bound estimates that serve to highlight the role of complementary policy reforms to support labor mobility and promote equality of opportunities in the labor market, especially for female workers.

Box 6.1 describes the effects that reductions in trade restrictions would have on employment and wages in Côte d'Ivoire. This country is showcased because of its

**Box 6.1     Wages and employment under AfCFTA in Côte d'Ivoire**

The final effect of the African Continental Free Trade Area (AfCFTA) agreement on wages in Côte d'Ivoire is driven by a series of factors. The most important are (1) the relative size of the reduction in trade barriers by economic activity; (2) the initial composition of labor in each economic activity; and (3) the future supply of labor by gender and skill (figures B6.1.1 and B6.1.2), not only in absolute terms in the country of interest, but also in relative terms to the rest of its trading partners. A global computable general equilibrium (CGE) model is uniquely capable of addressing these dynamic changes simultaneously in a consistent economic framework. Overall, changes in trade restrictiveness will increase the demand for certain varieties of products and increase the demand for the factors of production used to produce them.

As for the relative size of the reduction in trade barriers by economic activity, Côte d'Ivoire faces some of the highest trade restrictions in the continent. Over the simulation period (2020–35), however, it will also experience one of the largest reductions in tariffs and nontariff barriers, from 8 percent to 4 percent in tariffs and from 40 percent to 24 percent in nontariff barriers (NTBs) (see figures 4.4 and 4.5 in chapter 4). The textile and wearing apparel sector will experience the largest reduction in tariffs (from 10 percent to 3 percent), followed by energy-intensive manufacturing (from 5 percent to almost 0 percent) and manufactures, not elsewhere specified (from 4 percent

**Figure B6.1.1     Côte d'Ivoire: Labor composition by skill and gender: AfCFTA, 2035**

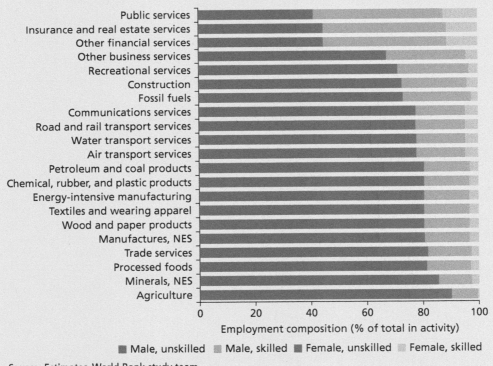

*Source:* Estimates, World Bank study team.

*Note:* AfCFTA = African Continental Free Trade Area.

*continued*

**Box 6.1** Wages and employment under AfCFTA in Côte d'Ivoire (*continued*)

**Figure B6.1.2** Côte d'Ivoire: Labor volumes by skill and gender, 2020 and 2035

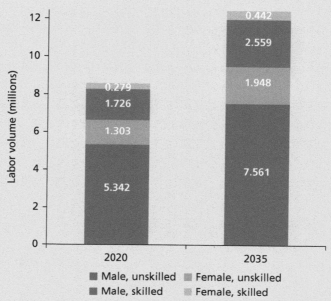

Source: Estimates, World Bank study team.

to 0.13 percent). Agriculture will experience a net decline of 4 percentage points in tariffs, from 24 percent to 20 percent. For NTBs, the sectors that benefit the most are chemical, rubber, and plastic products (with a decline in restrictions of 23 percentage points), energy-intensive manufacturing (−21 percentage points), and other business services (−19 percentage points).

Related to earlier points (2) and (3), figure B6.1.2 shows the final composition of employment by gender and skill under AfCFTA in 2035. Growth in the supply of labor by gender and skill is obtained from demographic projections (UN DESA 2019), assuming constant labor force participation rates. It follows that males would account for nearly 80 percent of employment across all industries. Nevertheless, the final composition of skills varies significantly across industries. Agriculture, which is among the industries that employ the largest proportion of males, is also the one with the highest intensity of unskilled labor.

Figures B6.1.3 and B6.1.4 show AfCFTA's effect on wages as the annual percentage point deviation from the baseline by industry and by type of worker, respectively. If AfCFTA is fully implemented, the wages of unskilled workers would grow 0.87 percentage points higher than the baseline. For skilled workers, wages would deviate less from the baseline (although from a higher base). Wages for skilled males would grow 0.68 percentage points higher than the baseline, whereas wages for skilled women would grow at a lower rate of 0.62 percentage points.

*continued*

**Box 6.1    Wages and employment under AfCFTA in Côte d'Ivoire (*continued*)**

Figure B6.1.3    Côte d'Ivoire: Effects of AfCFTA on wages by industry

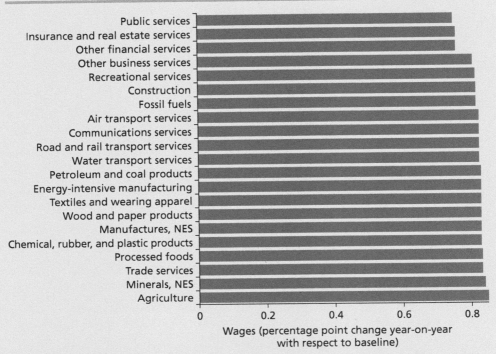

Source: Estimates, World Bank study team.

Note: AfCFTA = African Continental Free Trade Area; NES = not elsewhere specified.

Figure B6.1.4    Côte d'Ivoire: Effects of AfCFTA on wages by skill and gender

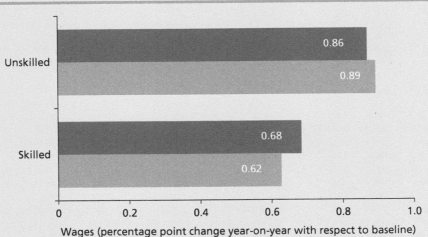

Source: Estimates, World Bank study team.

Note: AfCFTA = African Continental Free Trade Area.

relatively large reductions in trade barriers and highest expected welfare gains, although a similar analysis could be carried out for all countries in the simulation.

## NOTES

1. For the World Bank's harmonized list of countries with fragile situations, see https://www .worldbank.org/en/topic/fragilityconflictviolence/brief/harmonized-list-of-fragile-situations.

2. Poverty estimates are obtained by linking the results of a computable general equilibrium (CGE) model with a those of a simple global microeconomic model. The initial global distribution of per capita consumption/income is constructed using household-based data. Country-specific growth rates in real per capita household consumption from the macro CGE are fully transmitted to households assuming distribution neutrality. The number of poor is calculated by adjusting the total population of each country using the World Bank's population projections. A total of 163 countries are represented in the microeconomic model based on 146 harmonized, nationally representative household surveys obtained from the World Bank's Global Micro Database (GMD). Additional per capita consumption/income distributions for 17 countries were obtained from the World Bank's PovcalNet, an online analysis tool for global poverty monitoring.

3. With the exception of Djibouti and Libya (no data).

4. The World Bank now reports international poverty lines that are more closely related with national poverty standards. These poverty lines are set at US$1.90, US$3.20, and US$5.50, PPP-adjusted, for low-, lower-middle, and upper-middle-income countries, respectively.

5. By comparison, the World Bank estimated that 53.69 percent of the population of developing countries lived on less than US$5.50, PPP-adjusted, a day (US$3,369 million) in 2015.

6. There are still some minor differences in total employment attributable only to convergence issues.

7. There are still some minor differences in total employment attributable only to convergence issues.

8. See appendix G for a full description of the sectors.

9. Based on GTAP v.10 regions, these are the Democratic Republic of Congo, Rwanda, rest of Central Africa, Kenya, Uganda, rest of East Africa, Egypt, Morocco, rest of North Africa, Mozambique, Mauritius, Tanzania, South Africa, Zambia, Zimbabwe, rest of southern Africa, Côte d'Ivoire, Ghana, and Nigeria.

## REFERENCES

UN DESA. 2019. World Population Prospects 2019. United Nations. Department of Economic and Social Affairs. World Population Prospects 2019. https://population.un.org/wpp/Publications/Files /WPP2019_Highlights.pdf.

World Bank. 2018. "Poverty and Shared Prosperity 2018: Piecing Together the Poverty Puzzle." Washington, DC. https://doi.org/10.1596/978-1-4648-1330-6.

# 7 Sensitivity Analysis

The results of this analysis are sensitive to the key assumptions on the reduction of nontariff barriers (NTBs) in goods and services, as well as trade facilitation. In the central scenario for the African Continental Free Trade Area (AfCFTA), it is assumed that NTBs are reduced at the multilateral level. It is often argued that changes in NTBs benefit countries outside of the trade agreements to the same degree as the integrating countries. Indeed, some barriers are simply measures that do not discriminate across trading partners, and this view has been adopted in previous studies. In this analysis, however, two additional scenarios are considered:

- Scenario 1: (1) full liberalization of 97 percent of tariff lines as in the central AfCFTA scenario; (2) 50 percent reduction of NTBs in trade with all partners, with a cap of 50 percentage points; and (3) trade facilitation that reduces the costs of imports from all partners by half, although capped at 10 percentage points. This scenario removes reduction of NTBs that also benefit African exporters in AfCFTA and non-AfCFTA markets.
- Scenario 2: (1) full liberalization of 97 percent of tariff lines as in the central AfCFTA scenario; (2) 50 percent reduction of NTBs in trade with AfCFTA partners, with a cap of 50 percentage points; and (3) trade facilitation that reduces the costs of imports from AfCFTA partners by half, although capped at 10 percentage points.

Scenarios 1 and 2 are similar, but, in addition, all NTBs and trade facilitation measures reduce the trade cost only within the continent and not with respect to non-AfCFTA partners.

Under scenario 1, the continental welfare gains amount to about 5 percent. The countries that benefit the most under this scenario include the same countries that benefit the most under the central scenario, but overall gains are smaller because the costs of exporting remain unchanged.

Scenario 2 represents the lower bound of the estimate of gains. With no reduction in trade costs for non-AfCFTA partners, the continent would experience only the welfare gains of 1.2 percent. The biggest winners would be countries that trade the most within the continent such as Morocco, Namibia, and Senegal. The real income gains under all three scenarios are shown in table 7.1.

**Table 7.1**   Real income gains under three scenarios
*percent deviations with respect to baseline, 2035*

|  | AfCFTA | Scenario 1 | Scenario 2 |
| --- | --- | --- | --- |
| Total, Africa | 7 | 5 | 1 |
| Côte d'Ivoire | 13 | 8 | 4 |
| Zimbabwe | 11 | 6 | 3 |
| Kenya | 11 | 6 | 3 |
| Tanzania | 10 | 6 | 2 |
| Namibia | 10 | 6 | 6 |
| Congo, Dem. Rep. | 9 | 7 | 2 |
| Cameroon | 9 | 5 | 1 |
| Ethiopia | 9 | 4 | 1 |
| Morocco | 8 | 5 | 7 |
| Burkina Faso | 7 | 5 | 3 |
| Egypt, Arab Rep. | 7 | 5 | 0 |
| Mauritius | 6 | 3 | 2 |
| Ghana | 6 | 4 | 0 |
| Botswana | 6 | 3 | 1 |
| Tunisia | 6 | 3 | 3 |
| Senegal | 6 | 4 | 6 |
| Zambia | 5 | 2 | 2 |
| Nigeria | 4 | 4 | 0 |
| South Africa | 4 | 2 | 2 |
| Uganda | 3 | 2 | 1 |
| Madagascar | 3 | 2 | 0 |
| Rwanda | 3 | 2 | 0 |
| Mozambique | 2 | 0 | −1 |
| Malawi | 2 | 1 | 1 |

*Source:* Estimates, World Bank study team.

*Note:* AfCFTA = African Continental Free Trade Area.

# 8 Caveats

The quantitative results of this analysis are accompanied by some caveats. Reasons for an underestimation of the overall gains include:

- The baseline scenario has a relatively static assumption on trade preferences over time, including many "zero" flows in intracontinental bilateral trade in the reference year that remain zero throughout. Given the growth path, one might assume a growing preference for imports irrespective of price movements. The gains could be considerably larger with more open economies and with informal trade flows taken into consideration (see box 4.1 in chapter 4).

- Producers and consumers do benefit from lower prices, but also from an increase in product varieties. This so-called love-of-variety effect can have important impacts on consumer welfare. For producers as well, imports of key intermediate and capital goods can come embedded with technology that could lead to an increase in productivity, all else being equal.

- Rising exports could be associated with two additional impacts. First, exports in and of themselves may lead to rising productivity because exporters need to meet the quality and regulatory requirements of global markets. In addition, evidence suggests that rising exports tend to benefit higher-productivity firms, and this structural shift could lead to an increasing share of higher-productivity firms relative to lower-productivity firms that are producing for the domestic market. In addition to this structural shift, exporting firms may benefit from scale economies, which would be an additional boost for these firms.

- The model assumes constant returns to scale and perfect competition. Thus there are no procompetitive impacts from lowering trade barriers nor potentially pro-productivity impacts as more productive export-oriented firms gain market share.

- Most important, improving market conditions, competitiveness, and business sentiment would induce foreign direct investment in Africa, thereby leading to higher investment and accelerating imports of higher-technology intermediate and capital goods and improved management practices.

On the other hand, this analysis may overestimate the gains from trade for two reasons: the analysis ignores (1) the potential costs of lowering the nontariff barriers and the trade facilitation measures; and (2) the transitional costs associated with trade-related structural change such as employment shifts and potentially stranded assets such as capital.

Limitations associated with the use of microdata and the reconciliation with macroeconomic statistics should be considered. Nationally representative household surveys are incorporated in the computable general equilibrium (CGE) modeling framework to provide information related to the contribution of labor to value added, disaggregated by sector and type of worker. To incorporate this information, which is not available in national accounts statistics,[1] one must reconcile macrodata and microdata sources. This reconciliation must deal with the fact that (1) the aggregates obtained from microeconomic data do not add up to the aggregate statistics in national statistics; and (2) microeconomic data may not provide accurate information about some very small sectors.[2] Appendix B presents further details on the construction of the microbased statistics and the validation process. Overall, the microdata used in this study are not meant to provide, especially for the general public, timely and accurate labor statistics. Rather, they are meant to provide a detailed representation of relative labor conditions that exist between and within countries within the context of general equilibrium modeling.

## NOTES

1. Most countries in Africa now have the technical capacity to gather and document national accounts statistics, and these statistics—along with ancillary data from central banks, customs authorities, and other agencies—usually provide a fair, if not always accurate and timely, macro picture of the economy.

2. For example, a small sampling size in the survey design may not be able to capture enough observations for very small sectors or groups of people, which can lead to unreliable statistics. Another consideration is that a household survey is bounded to recover information about individuals within its sampling framework, excluding the homeless or individuals living in refugee camps. Finally, an emerging restriction is no response, which affects in a greater proportion the wealthier segments of the population.

# Appendix A: Data Preparation on Disaggregated Labor Volumes and Wages

The computable general equilibrium (CGE) model requires internationally comparable statistics on labor remuneration and employment volume to be disaggregated by workers' skill level and gender. This appendix covers the technical aspects of the construction of disaggregated labor value-added statistics for each country and economic activity in the Global Trade Analysis Project Version 10 (GTAP 10) database. It also provides an overall perspective on the data set's underlying advantages and its caveats.

Disaggregated data on labor remuneration and employment volume were generated using harmonized household surveys obtained from the World Bank's International Income Distribution Data Set (I2D2)[1] and labor statistics obtained from the Luxembourg Income Study (LIS) database, supplemented with disaggregated earnings and employment distribution provided by the International Labour Organization (ILO) and other national employment statistics compiled by the World Bank. Figure A.1 shows the general structure of the data processing. The disaggregated labor database is consistent with the GTAP 10 database for the base year 2014 (also see appendix G). It contains labor volume and remuneration disaggregated by gender and two skill levels.[2] The database includes data for each of the 141 GTAP 10 regions and 65 economic activities.[3]

Internationally comparable disaggregated statistics on wages and employment appear to be only available at the one-digit International Standard Industrial Classification (ISIC) level.[4] Thus further disaggregation required mining each survey's metadata[5] to gather information about national industry and occupation classifications. The construction process begins by collecting initial labor and monthly wage statistics based on 92 nationally representative, preharmonized household surveys (see table A.1 for the complete list of surveys). The exploited variables include individual and household characteristics; demographic information (age, gender); level of education or years of schooling; labor force and employment status; industry and occupation original codes; and (self-reported) wages in local currency units (LCUs) and unit of last payment. Based on this information, industry and occupation variables are then reharmonized to the highest level possible using ISIC (Rev. 4) and International Standard Classification of Occupations (ISCO) (08) codes, respectively. Finally, all

**Figure A.1**   Procedure for establishing wage and employment volume

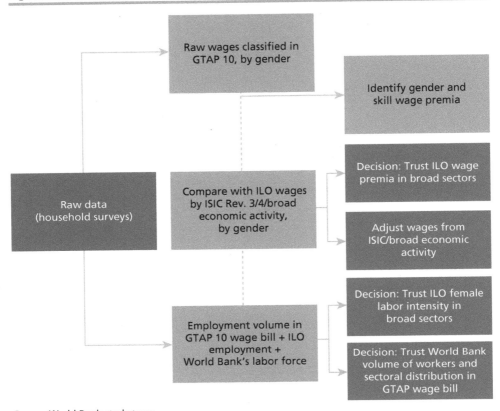

*Source:* World Bank study team.
*Note:* GTAP = Global Trade Analysis Project; ILO = International Labour Organzation; ISIC = International Standard Industrial Classification.

industry codes are transferred from ISIC (Rev. 4) to the broader 65-sector GTAP 10 activity codes.

Household surveys claim their samples are nationally representative and that the surveys replicate, at some subnational level of disaggregation, features such as gender and age composition and employment distribution across broad economic activities. Nevertheless, the accuracy of statistics based on survey data is bounded by a survey's sampling design.[6] Even though each worker in a household survey is mapped to a specific GTAP activity, the sampling nature of each survey cannot guarantee that all disaggregated sectors are fully represented. Another important caveat of household survey data is related to some level of inaccuracy, especially with variables that are difficult to recall such as wages for the self-employed.

These problems are solved by validation through external data. The overall strategy is to use the relative wages by skill and gender for each of the 65 GTAP economic activities (obtained from household surveys), ensuring that the sum of wages is aligned with

Table A.1    Household surveys used for the construction of wage bill data

| Country name | Country survey | | Year |
| --- | --- | --- | --- |
| | Code | Survey abbreviation | |
| **East Asia and Pacific** | | | |
| Australia | AUS | HILDA | 2015 |
| Cambodia | KHM | CLFCLS | 2012 |
| China | CHN | CGSS | 2013 |
| Fiji | FJI | HIES | 2008 |
| Indonesia | IDN | SAKERNAS | 2009 |
| Mongolia | MNG | LFS | 2013 |
| Philippines | PHL | LFS | 2014 |
| Solomon Islands | SLB | HIES | 2005 |
| Thailand | THA | HSES | 2011 |
| Timor-Leste | TMP | LFS | 2010 |
| Vietnam | VNM | LFS | 2010 |
| **Europe and Central Asia** | | | |
| Austria | AUT | SILC | 2013 |
| Azerbaijan | AZE | AMSSW | 2015 |
| Belarus | BLR | LFS | 2016 |
| Czech Republic | CZE | SILC | 2013 |
| Denmark | DNK | Law_Model | 2013 |
| Estonia | EST | HBS | 2004 |
| Finland | FIN | IDS_SILC | 2013 |
| Georgia | GEO | HIS | 2013 |
| Germany | DEU | GSOEP | 2014 |
| Greece | GRC | SILC | 2013 |
| Hungary | HUN | HNS | 2008 |
| Kosovo | KSV | LFS | 2014 |
| Lithuania | LTU | HBS | 2008 |
| Luxembourg | LUX | PSELLIII_SIL | 2013 |
| Moldova | MDA | LFS | 2015 |
| Montenegro | MNE | LFS | 2011 |

*continued*

**Table A.1**    Household surveys used for the construction of wage bill data *(continued)*

| Country name | Country survey | | Year |
| | Code | Survey abbreviation | |
|---|---|---|---|
| Poland | POL | HBS | 2011 |
| Russian Federation | RUS | RMLS | 2016 |
| Slovak Republic | SVK | SILC | 2013 |
| Slovenia | SVN | HBS | 2004 |
| Switzerland | CHE | SILC | 2013 |
| Tajikistan | TJK | JMSC | 2013 |
| Turkey | TUR | HLFS | 2015 |
| United Kingdom | GBR | SILC | 2013 |
| **Latin America and the Caribbean** | | | |
| Argentina | ARG | EPHC_2 | 2014 |
| Bolivia | BOL | EH | 2015 |
| Brazil | BRA | PNAD | 2015 |
| Chile | CHL | CASEN | 2015 |
| Colombia | COL | GEIH | 2014 |
| Costa Rica | CRI | ENAHO | 2012 |
| Dominican Republic | DOM | ENFT | 2015 |
| Ecuador | ECU | ENEMDU | 2015 |
| El Salvador | SLV | EHPM | 2014 |
| Haiti | HTI | EEEI | 2007 |
| Honduras | HND | EPHPM | 2014 |
| Mexico | MEX | ENIGH | 2010 |
| Nicaragua | NIC | EMNV | 2014 |
| Peru | PER | ENAHO | 2015 |
| Uruguay | URY | ECH | 2015 |
| **Middle East and North Africa** | | | |
| Djibouti | DJI | EDESIC | 2015 |
| Egypt, Arab Rep. | EGY | ELMPS | 2005 |
| Iraq | IRQ | HSES | 2012 |
| Jordan | JOR | LFS | 2016 |

*continued*

**Table A.1**  Household surveys used for the construction of wage bill data *(continued)*

| Country name | Country survey | | Year |
| --- | --- | --- | --- |
| | Code | Survey abbreviation | |
| Lebanon | LBN | LBN | 2011 |
| Morocco | MAR | ENSLE | 2009 |
| Tunisia | TUN | HBS | 2010 |
| **South Asia** | | | |
| Afghanistan | AFG | ALCS | 2013 |
| Bangladesh | BGD | HIES | 2010 |
| Bhutan | BTN | BLSS | 2017 |
| India | IND | NSS_SCH10 | 2011 |
| Maldives | MDV | HIES | 2009 |
| Nepal | NPL | LSS | 2010 |
| Pakistan | PAK | LFS | 2014 |
| Sri Lanka | LKA | HIES | 2016 |
| **Sub-Saharan Africa** | | | |
| Angola | AGO | CENSUS | 2014 |
| Botswana | BWA | BCWIS | 2009 |
| Eswatini | SWZ | HIES | 2000 |
| Ethiopia | ETH | UEUS | 2016 |
| Gambia, The | GMB | IHS | 2015 |
| Kenya | KEN | IHBS | 2005 |
| Lesotho | LSO | HBS | 2010 |
| Malawi | MWI | LES | 2013 |
| Mali | MLI | EPAM | 2010 |
| Mauritius | MUS | HBS | 2012 |
| Mozambique | MOZ | IOF | 2014 |
| Namibia | NAM | LFS | 2014 |
| Niger | NER | ECVMA | 2014 |
| Rwanda | RWA | EICV | 2013 |
| São Tomé and Príncipe | STP | IOF | 2010 |
| Seychelles | SYC | HBS | 2006 |

*continued*

**Table A.1**   Household surveys used for the construction of wage bill data *(continued)*

| Country name | Country survey | | Year |
| | Code | Survey abbreviation | |
| --- | --- | --- | --- |
| Sierra Leone | SLE | LFS | 2016 |
| Somalia | SOM | HFS | 2016 |
| South Africa | ZAF | QLFS_Q1 | 2017 |
| Sudan | SDN | NBHS | 2009 |
| Uganda | UGA | UNHS | 2016 |
| Zambia | ZMB | LCMS | 2015 |
| Zimbabwe | ZWE | LFS | 2011 |
| North America | | | |
| United States | USA | CPS | 2018 |

*Source:* World Bank study team.

the aggregated sectors (21 sectors at the ISIC Rev. 4 one-digit level) of the International Labour Organization and that employment and labor value added correspond with national statistics and GTAP, respectively. The databases used for external validation include (1) ILO employment and monthly earnings data;[7] (2) national data on employment (compiled by the World Bank); and (3) GTAP 10 capital and labor value-added data. The final database contains the share of value added of labor for each type of worker, activity, and region. Because it represents labor remuneration multiplied by employment volume, it is straightforward to calculate labor volumes by simply dividing the wage bill by average wages.

## NOTES

1. I2D2 is a unique database compiled by the World Bank. It includes more than 1,600 nationally representative household surveys for 140 countries. Despite the obvious limitations of such a large harmonization effort (such as compatibility issues due to different survey designs and currency conversions from local to international), the I2D2 data set is the largest available source of micro-level individual employment characteristics. A detailed description of the source can be found in Gindling and Newhouse (2014).

2. In this analysis, nine-plus years of schooling defines a "skilled worker" in low- and lower-middle-income countries. For upper-middle and high-income countries, a threshold of 13 and more years of schooling is used. Income levels are based on the World Bank's official classification of countries based on gross domestic product (GDP) per capita in purchasing power parity (PPP) dollars (Atlas Method).

3. Complete details of the GTAP 10 database can be found at https://www.gtap.agecon.purdue.edu /databases/v10/index.aspx.

4. Twenty-one sectors in ISIC Rev. 4 and 17 sectors in ISIC Rev. 3.1.

5.  Although this process involved examining the quality of survey data, most efforts were devoted to gathering metadata about national classification systems. In most cases, countries based their national systems on international standards, but they adjusted their classifications to their own needs. Concordance tables and international mapping in the form of metadata were thus created for this project and are available upon request. The resulting metadata sheet contains information for 78 I2D2 and 15 LI.S. household surveys that represent more than 70 percent of global GDP and 80 percent of the global population.

6.  The use of survey instruments comes with other problems as well. In recent years, falling response rates and data errors have compromised the usefulness of some surveys and resulted in lower-quality data. For example, respondents in more affluent groups tend to give inaccurate information about their personal finances, especially wages (Meyer, Mok, and Sullivan 2015).

7.  The ILO database compiles the largest set of labor-specific statistics with global coverage. It includes data for 149 countries. The ILO publishes three tables that can be disaggregated by gender, including "Mean nominal monthly earnings of employees by sex and economic activity," "Employees by sex and economic activity (thousands)," and "Employment distribution by economic activity (by sex)." Although some of this information is gender-disaggregated specific tabulations with cleaned and reasonable data for every year (and wages in the local currency and U.S. dollars), some regions or years are not available for the full data or are only harmonized to board economic activities.

# REFERENCES

Gindling, T. H., and David Newhouse. 2014. "Self-Employment in the Developing World." *World Development* 56: 313–31. https://doi.org/10.1016/j.worlddev.2013.03.003.

Meyer, Bruce D., Wallace K. C. Mok, and James X. Sullivan. 2015. "Household Surveys in Crisis." *Journal of Economic Perspectives* 29 (4): 199–226. https://doi.org/10.1257/jep.29.4.199.

# Appendix B: Summary Description of the GIDD Model

In the microsimulation model, the ultimate focus of analysis is the evolution of the distribution of the welfare in different scenarios. Starting from base year $t$, the income or expenditure[1] ($Y_{i,t}$) of each individual living in a household can be modeled as a function of (1) its own characteristics and the household members' characteristics or assets (endowments) ($x$); (2) the market reward for those characteristics ($\beta$); (3) the intensity in how those endowments are used as captured by a set of parameters $\lambda$ defining labor force participation and occupation status ($L|\lambda$); and (4) the unobservable components ($\varepsilon$), expressed as

$$Y_{i,t} = f(x_{i,t}, \beta_t, (L_{i,t} | \lambda_t), \varepsilon_{i,t}). \tag{B.1}$$

The income distribution $D$ for a population of $N$ individuals (or households) in the base year $t$ can be represented by the vector $\{Y_{1,t} \dots Y_{i,t} \dots Y_{N,t}\}$, where each $Y_{i,t}$ can be defined in terms of endowments, prices, labor status, and unobservables to yield

$$D_t = \{Y_{1,t} \dots Y_{N,t}\} = \{f(X_{i,t}, \beta_t, (L_{i,t}|\lambda_t), \varepsilon_{i,t}) \dots f(X_{N,t}, \beta_t (L_{N,t}|\lambda_t), \varepsilon_{N,t})\}. \tag{B.2}$$

How does this distribution change dynamically, such as from year $t$ to year $t + k$? This framework allows one to distinguish two sources that affect the dynamic change of distribution $D$, both of which are relevant to assessment of the distributive impact of the African Continental Free Trade Area (AfCFTA). The first source consists of the changes in parameter $\beta$ or $\lambda$—namely, the market rewards for the characteristics (or assets) $X$ and parameters affecting occupational decisions. This means, for example, that inequality for distribution $D$ can go down if the skill premia $\beta_{skill}/\beta_{unskill}$ is reduced, or if a change in labor demand in sectors with higher wages (a change in $\lambda$) affects the decision by some individuals working in sectors with lower wages to move to higher-paying sectors. The second source of a dynamic shift is represented by changes in the distribution of individual and household characteristics ($X$). Alterations in the structure of the population in terms of age and education by gender, as well as changes in the size and composition of households, will all affect the distribution of income of that population.[2]

Both sources of distributional change matter to the impacts of AfCFTA. Defining the contrasting values of endowments, prices, and labor status to build the two $\hat{D}$s can be quite challenging, especially when done for many countries. To do so, one begins with a distribution of earnings from labor by sector and skill ($y_{s,e}$) in the macrodata, defining a set of wage gaps so that

$$g_{s,e} = \frac{y_{g,s,e}}{y_{f,1,1}} - 1 \qquad (B.3)$$

and a similar set of wage gaps for the macroeconomic counterfactual scenario so that

$$\hat{g}_{s,e} = \frac{\hat{y}_{x,s,e}}{\hat{y}_{f,1,1}} - 1, \qquad (B.4)$$

where $y_{f,1,1}$ is the average earnings from the labor of female unskilled workers in agriculture, and $\hat{y}_{f,1,1}$ and $\hat{y}_{x,s,e}$ are their predicted values from the computable general equilibrium (CGE) model in the counterfactual scenario. All right-hand values in equation (B.3) are known data in the CGE model benchmark data set, and all right-hand values in equation (B.4) are known values in the CGE model simulations.

The microdata will also have a set of wage premia that in general will differ from the CGE data. Analogous to equations (B.3) and (B.4), one defines

$$g'_{s,e} = \frac{y'_{x,s,e}}{y'_{f,1,1}} - 1 \qquad (B.5)$$

and

$$\hat{g}'_{s,e} = \frac{\hat{y}'_{x,s,e}}{\hat{y}'_{f,1,1}} - 1, \qquad (B.6)$$

where $g'_{s,e}$ is the wage premia based on averages by skill group and sector in the household data; $y'_{s,e}$ is the average earnings of labor in sector $s$, skill group $e$, and gender $x$ based on the household data; $y'_{f,1,1}$ is the average earnings of female unskilled labor in agriculture based on the household data; and $\hat{g}'$ is the predicted value at the household level as a result of the policy change. All right-hand values of equation (B.5) are known from the initial household data. One calculates $g'_{x,s,e}$ by means of

$$\hat{g}'_{x,s,e} = g'_{x,s,e} \frac{\hat{g}'_{x,s,e}}{g_{x,s,e}}. \qquad (B.7)$$

It is possible to calculate the left-hand side of equation (B.7) because the three values on the right-hand side are known from equations (B.3), (B.4), and (B.5). Equation (B.7) implies that even if initial wages differ between the CGE and micromodels, the percentage change in the wage gaps will be consistent across the two models. By passing on percentage changes in wage premia by type of worker instead of percentage changes in wages, the possibility of wage gaps moving in opposite directions in the macrodata and in the household data is eliminated. Within each group of workers, distributional changes occur, but on average for any group of workers the relative wages for each type of worker are constrained to be consistent with the corresponding growth rates from the CGE model.

Given the known values in equations (B.3)–(B.7), and defining average wages for female unskilled labor in agriculture as numeraire in the Global Income Distribution Dynamics (GIDD) so that $y'_{f,1,1} = y'_{f,1,1}$, it is possible to calculate the percentage changes in average wage income in sector $s$, skill level $e$, and gender $x$ that are consistent with the wage gaps expressed in equation (B.7) so that

$$\hat{y}'_{g,s,e}/y'_{g,s,e}.$$ (B.8)

Equation (B.8) operates only on labor income. To adjust the microdata so that the weighted average percentage change in the per capita income/consumption across all households matches the change in real consumption per capita in the CGE model, one must carry out the following adjustment:

- Define $Y$ as real per capita income calculated from the CGE model in the benchmark and $\hat{Y}$ as its predicted value in the CGE model simulation.
- Define $y'_h = \Sigma_i \varepsilon_h y'_{i,h}/n_h$ as the per capita income of household $h$ in the benchmark equilibrium, where $y'_{i,h}$ is the income of the $i$th member of household $h$, and $n$ is equal to the size of household $h$.
- Similarly, define $\lambda\hat{y}'_h = \Sigma_i \in_h \lambda\hat{y}'_{i,h}/n_h$, where $\hat{y}'_{i,h}$ and $\lambda\hat{y}'_{i,h}$ are the unadjusted and adjusted values, respectively, of the income of the $i$th member of household $h$ in the counterfactual of the micromodel.
- Then define $Y'$ as the weighted average value of real per capita income across all households—that is,

$$\Sigma'_h V_h \gamma'_h = Y',$$ (B.9)

where $V_h$ is the weight of household $h$ in aggregate income in the benchmark. Correspondingly,

$$\Sigma'_h \omega_h \lambda\hat{\gamma}'_h = \hat{Y}'$$ (B.10)

is the weighted average per capita income value in the policy simulation, where $\Sigma_h u_h = 1$, $\Sigma_h \omega_h = 1$, and $\lambda$ is a scalar.

Equations (B.9) and (B.10) allow for different household weights because the weights of the households will typically change over time. So that the percentage change in the aggregate value of household income is consistent with the CGE model, $\hat{Y}$ is constrained by equation (B.11),

$$\hat{Y}' = Y' \frac{Y'}{Y}.$$ (B.11)

This constraint is implemented in a distribution-neutral way—that is, all household income is adjusted in the counterfactual by a scalar $\lambda$ so that per capita household income equals $\lambda \hat{Y}'_h$. As a result, $\lambda$ can be defined by

$$\lambda \sum_h \omega_h \hat{\gamma}_h = Y' \frac{Y'}{Y}.$$ (B.12)

Despite the fact that the GIDD ignores other forms of income, such as capital income, this transformation guarantees consistency between the weighted average household income assessment and the CGE model assessment. For households that receive labor income, which is the main focus of this work, the assumption should be reasonably accurate. The margin of error for wealthier households is larger. But for these households, it is skilled labor rather than unskilled labor that tends to be more important. Bussolo, De Hoyos, and Medvedev (2010) have noted a tendency for skilled wage and returns to capital to be correlated.

Finally, macroeconomic estimates of changes in agricultural and nonagricultural prices are distributed across heterogeneous households using the following method. The initial per capita monetary income of household $h$, $\gamma'_h$, and the purchasing power of household $h$, $\gamma^r_h$, are defined as the ratio of its monetary income divided by a household-specific price index capturing the household's consumption patterns in terms of food and nonfood expenditures so that

$$\gamma^r_h = \frac{\gamma'_h}{P_h} = \frac{\gamma'_h}{\alpha_h P_f + (1-\alpha_h) P_{nf}},$$ (B.13)

where $P_f$ and $P_{nf}$ are food and nonfood price indices, and $\alpha_h$ is the proportion of the budget of household $h$ spent on food.

The $\alpha_h$ parameter in the denominator of the right-hand side of equation (B.13) can be estimated with household data using

$$\alpha_h = \beta_0 + \beta_1 \ln(\gamma'_h) + e_h,$$ (B.14)

where $e_h$ is a vector of household-specific errors that are assumed to be distributed with $E(e_h) = 0$ and $V(e_h) = \sigma^2$. Assuming that the estimated parameters $\beta_0$ and $\beta_1$ remain constant, the new budget share spent on food for household $h$, $\alpha'h$, at the counterfactual per capita income, $\lambda \hat{y}'_h$ can be obtained from

$$\hat{\alpha}'_h = \hat{\beta}_0 + \hat{\beta}_1 \ln(\lambda \hat{\gamma}'_h) + \hat{e}_h.$$ (B.15)

The changes in real per capita incomes brought about by a change in the relative prices of food versus nonfood can be approximated by the linear expression

$$\hat{\gamma}^r_h = \frac{\lambda \hat{\gamma}'_h}{\hat{\alpha}'_h P'_f + (1-\hat{\alpha}'_h) P'_{nf}},$$ (B.16)

where $\hat{y}_h^r$ in equation (B.16) is the real per capita income adjusted for changes in the relative prices of food versus nonfood, and $\hat{y}_h^r$ is the counterfactual measure of real per capita income of household $h$ for the analysis of poverty and shared prosperity.

## NOTES

1. This analysis uses the household consumption expenditure wherever available and income when the consumption expenditure is not available such as in many countries in Latin America and the Caribbean. The variables consumption and income are used interchangeably given the qualification. Clearly, income dispersion will tend to be higher than consumption dispersion within countries, and having a uniform welfare variable for all countries would be better. However, this limitation affects all comparable studies of global income distribution—see, for example, Lakner and Milanovic (2013) and World Bank (2016).

2. These two sources of dynamic change are not independent of one another, and in the real world, they are simultaneously determined. The problems encountered in estimating and running a fully simultaneous microsimulation framework are discussed in more detail in Bourguignon and Bussolo (2013).

## REFERENCES

Bourguignon, François, and Maurizio Bussolo. 2013. "Income Distribution in Computable General Equilibrium Modeling." In *Handbook of Computable General Equilibrium Modeling*, 1: 1383–437. Amsterdam: Elsevier.

Bussolo, Maurizio, Rafael E. De Hoyos, and Denis Medvedev. 2010. "Economic Growth and Income Distribution: Linking Macro-Economic Models with Household Survey Data at the Global Level." *International Journal of Microsimulation* 3 (1): 92–103.

Lakner, Christoph, and Branko Milanovic. 2013. "Global Income Distribution: From the Fall of the Berlin Wall to the Great Recession." Policy Research Working Paper, World Bank, Washington, DC. https://doi.org/10.1596/1813-9450-6719.

World Bank. 2016. *Poverty and Shared Prosperity 2016: Taking on Inequality.* Washington, DC: World Bank. https://doi.org/10.1596/978-1-4648-0958-3.

# Appendix C: Deep Commitments in African Regional Economic Communities, Legal Texts

What follows are references to the legal texts of the African Continental Free Trade Area (AfCFTA) and the African subregional regional trade agreements (RTAs).

## EAST AFRICAN COMMUNITY (EAC)

- EAC Treaty—Treaty for the Establishment of the East African Community, http://rtais.wto.org/rtadocs/94/TOA/English/EAC20TREATY.pdf
- Protocol on the Establishment of the EAC Common Market, http://eacj.org /wp-content/uploads/2012/08/Common-Market-Protocol.pdf

## EAC TREATY

- Chapter 11—reference to protocol
- Chapter 12—cooperation in investment
- Chapter 13—technical barriers to trade
- Chapter 14—movement of capital (Article 86)
- Chapter 15—services
- Chapter 18—sanitary and phytosanitary measures
- Chapter 19—environment
- Article 75—customs

## PROTOCOL ON THE ESTABLISHMENT OF THE EAC COMMON MARKET

- Part C—free movement of goods
- Part F—services
- Part G—free movement of capital
- Article 29— investment

- Articles 33, 34, 36—competition
- Article 35—public procurement
- Article 40—environment
- Article 43—intellectual property rights
- Article 34—subsidies = state aid
- Part D—labor

## COMMON MARKET FOR EAST AND SOUTH AFRICA (COMESA)

- COMESA Treaty (1994), https://www.comesacompetition.org/wp-content/uploads/2016/03/COMESA_Treaty.pdf

## COMESA TREATY

- Chapter 6—customs (Article 58, among others). See also Chapter 7.
- Chapter 6—trade liberalization (goods)
- Article 51—antidumping
- Article 52—state aid
- Articles 53—exceptions to levying of countervailing duty
- Article 54—cooperation in investigation of dumping and subsidies
- Article 55—competition
- Article 81—movement of capital
- Chapter 15—technical barriers to trade
- Chapter 16—environment
- Chapter 26—investment
- Article 86—export duties
- Chapter 6—includes trade in services = General Agreement on Trade in Services. See also Chapter 11.
- Article 132—sanitary and phytosanitary measures
- Chapter 28—labor. See also Article 143.1(b).

## SOUTH AFRICAN DEVELOPMENT COMMUNITY (SADC)

- SADC Treaty (1992), https://www.wipo.int/edocs/lexdocs/treaties/en/sadc/trt_sadc.pdf
- Protocol on Trade (August 1996), https://wipolex.wipo.int/en/text/203430

## PROTOCOL ON TRADE

- Part 2—trade in goods
- Article 5—export taxes

- Part 3—customs (Article 13)
- Article 16—sanitary and phytosanitary measures
- Article 17—technical barriers to trade
- Article 18—antidumping
- Article 19—subsidies and countervailing measures
- Part 5—investment
- Article 23—General Agreement on Trade in Services
- Article 24—intellectual property rights
- Article 25—competition

## ECONOMIC COMMUNITY OF WEST AFRICAN STATES (ECOWAS)

- ECOWAS Treaty, https://www.ecowas.int/wp-content/uploads/2015/01/Revised -treaty.pdf

## ECOWAS TREATY

- Chapter VI—environment
- Article 35—trade liberalization
- Articles 36, 46—customs
- Article 42—dumping
- Article 53—movement of capital
- References to services trade throughout the treaty—General Agreement on Trade in Services

## WEST AFRICAN ECONOMIC AND MONETARY UNION (WAEMU)

- WAEMU Treaty, http://www.uemoa.int/fr/system/files/fichier_article /traitreviseuemoa.pdf

## WAEMU TREATY

- Articles 76, 77—trade in goods
- Articles 88–90—competition
- Article 77—export taxes
- Various references to services trade throughout the agreement—General Agreement on Trade in Services
- Articles 76, 79—movement of capital

## SOUTH AFRICAN CUSTOMS UNION (SACU)

- SACU Agreement, http://sacu.int/docs/agreements/2017/SACU-Agreement.pdf

## SACU AGREEMENT

- Part 5—trade liberalization
- Article 23—customs
- Article 28—technical barriers to trade
- Article 30—sanitary and phytosanitary measures
- Articles 40, 41—competition

## ECONOMIC AND MONETARY COMMUNITY OF CENTRAL AFRICA (CEMAC)

- CEMAC Treaty, http://rtais.wto.org/UI/CRShowRTAIDCard.aspx?rtaid=95

## CEMAC TREATY

- Article 13—trade liberalization
- Articles 23–25—competition
- Section V—environment
- Article 14(o)—export taxes
- Articles 13, 23—state aid
- Article 19—antidumping
- Article 17—technical barriers to trade and sanitary and phytosanitary measures
- Various references to services—General Agreement on Trade in Services
- Article 28—movement of capital

## AFRICAN CONTINENTAL FREE TRADE AREA (AfCFTA)

- AfCFTA Treaty, https://au.int/sites/default/files/treaties/36437-treaty-consolidated _text_on_cfta_-_en.pdf

## AfCFTA TREATY

- Article 6—goods, services, investment, intellectual property rights, competition
- Protocol on Trade in Goods
  - Article 10—export duties
  - Articles 14, 15—customs
  - Article 17—antidumping and countervailing measures
  - Article 21—technical barriers to trade
  - Article 22—sanitary and phytosanitary measures
  - Article 25—state trading enterprises

- Protocol on Trade in Services—General Agreement on Trade in Services
  - Articles 11, 12—competition
  - Article 13—payments, transfers (movement of capital)
  - Article 2.4—carve-out for public procurement ("Procurement by governmental agencies purchased for governmental purposes and not with a view to commercial re-sale are excluded from the scope of this Protocol")

# Appendix D: Literature Review on the Impacts of AfCFTA

The existing literature on the quantitative impacts of the African Continental Free Trade Area (AfCFTA) has focused mainly on evaluating the effects of reducing tariffs and nontariff barriers (NTBs), as well as trade facilitation measures, on African welfare.

Computable general equilibrium (CGE) modeling relying on the Global Trade Analysis Project (GTAP) as a database is broadly used in studies to evaluate the impacts of the shocks of tariff reductions, with some studies using TASTE (Tariff Analytical and Simulation Tool for Economists) for the specific cuts in tariff lines. Chauvin, Ramos, and Porto (2016) apply the MIRAGE-e CGE to study the impacts of tariff, NTB, and trade cost reductions. The authors also apply microsimulations to evaluate the effects of price and wage changes on the welfare of households in six Sub-Saharan countries.

Vanzetti, Peters, and Knebel (2018) apply a standard GTAP model. To measure the quantitative impacts of the AfCFTA, they applied three shocks to the model: (1) full elimination of tariffs; (2) tariff elimination with exemptions for 5 percent of sensitive products; and (3) NTB reduction without tariff reduction. Chauvin, Ramos, and Porto (2016) opt for a more incremental approach, with all simulations in the first stage of the study running until 2027. They first eliminate all tariffs on agricultural goods, and then on all manufactured goods. The third shock consists of adding a 50 percent reduction in NTBs. Finally, they apply a 30 percent reduction in transaction costs to all goods.

The results of these studies reveal that by eliminating all the applied tariffs, the African continent would register an annual increase in trade of up to US$3.6 billion. The demand for labor, both skilled and unskilled, will experience a sharp increase, especially in countries such as Kenya, Nigeria, and South Africa. However, these results are asymmetric throughout the continent with Angola, Nigeria, and South Africa being the main winners. In some countries, there may even be a reduction in welfare in the medium and long run—for example, in Burkina Faso, Malawi, Mozambique, and Rwanda when agricultural tariffs are eliminated (Chauvin, Ramos, and Porto 2016). In the scenario with an exemption of 5 percent of sensitive products, the effect is a reduction in the gains for trade by more than 60 percent.

Abrego et al. (2019) demonstrate that the size of the potential gains in allocative efficiency that may be obtained from AfCFTA is deeply dependent on the degree of openness, initial level of trade barriers, and the strength of the initial intra-Africa trade ties of each country. The study also shows how the continent can have the biggest benefits by reducing the NTBs, together with lowering tariffs. The increase in welfare in this scenario will be 2.1 percent compared with the baseline, with all countries enjoying welfare increases, and nine of them with gains of 5 percent or more.

The microsimulations applied by Chauvin, Ramos, and Porto (2016) point to the heterogeneity of the impacts on welfare. In some countries such Burkina Faso, the benefits will help the poor more, whereas in Cameroon and Nigeria, the rich will gain more. Male-headed households will have better gains in Nigeria, in contrast with Burkina Faso, Côte d'Ivoire, and Ethiopia, where female-headed households will be the biggest winners. Rural households will benefit more in Côte d'Ivoire, whereas urban households will earn more in Cameroon, Ethiopia, and Madagascar.

In addition to the gains already mentioned and observed such as in the demand for labor and welfare (especially if there is a reduction in NTBs), Africa will derive other benefits from AfCFTA as well. Increasing intra-Africa trade relative to trade with the rest of world will render intra-Africa trade more resilient to global price shocks. African countries will also trade among themselves a more diverse set of goods and products because trade with nonregional partners tends to be very concentrated and focused on primary commodities. Finally, a deeper regional integration effort such as AfCFTA also creates an opportunity for a further reduction of barriers to trade, and it has the potential to generate economies of scale (Ahmed et al. 2018).

CGE simulations by the African Development Bank reinforce the conclusions in the rest of the literature and complement it by adding further simulations that implement the trade facilitation agreement (ADB 2019). The additional set of scenarios indicates that the biggest gains for most of the regions materialize when tariffs and nontariff barriers are removed, the trade facilitation agreement on a most-favored-nation basis is implemented, and tariffs and nontariff barriers to other developing countries are reduced by 50 percent. This scenario reveals an increase in market access in other developing countries and raises total African exports by 57 percent, which translates into gains of 4.5 percent of Africa's gross domestic product (GDP) over the baseline (or an additional US$31 billion), equivalent to the total gain of US$134 billion. The Central Africa region reaps the most benefits, followed by North, West, and East Africa.

The results from the literature show that under liberalization scenarios, where there is a reduction in NTBs and an improvement in trade facilitation conditions, there is a much more substantial increase in trade and welfare than in scenarios in which there are only tariff reductions. For example, the costs associated with sanitary and phytosanitary measures and technical barriers to trade can be reduced by a quarter, and traditional barriers, such as quotas, can be fully eliminated without losses for any country. A gain of up to US$20 billion can be obtained by reducing the trade distortion effect of the NTBs, with the biggest winners being the Arab Republic of Egypt, Kenya, and South Africa (Vanzetti, Peters, and Knebel 2018).

# REFERENCES

Abrego, Lisandro, Maria Alejandra Amado, Tunc Gursoy, Garth Nicholls, and Hector Perez-Saiz. 2019. "The African Continental Free Trade Agreement: Welfare Gains Estimates from a General Equilibrium Model." https://www.imf.org/en/Publications/WP/Issues/2019/06/07/The-African -Continental-Free-Trade-Agreement-Welfare-Gains-Estimates-from-a-General-46881.

ADB (African Development Bank). 2019. *African Economic Outlook 2019*. Abidjan, Côte d'Ivoire: ADB.

Ahmed, Lesley, Renee Berry, Mark Brininstool, and Jennifer Catalano. 2018. *U.S. Trade and Investment with Sub-Saharan Africa: Recent Developments*. Washington, DC: U.S. International Trade Commission.

Chauvin, Depetris Nicolas, M. Priscila Ramos, and Guido Porto. 2016. "Trade, Growth, and Welfare Impacts of the CFTA in Africa." Working paper, International Household Survey Network. http://hesso.tind.io/record/2006/files/Depetris-Chauvin_2017_trade_growth_welfare.pdf.

Vanzetti, David, Ralf Peters, and Christian Knebel. 2018. "Non-Tariff Measures: Lifting CFTA and ACP Trade to the Next Level." UNCTAD Research Paper No. 14, United Nations Conference on Trade and Development, Geneva. http://unctad.org/en/PublicationsLibrary/ser-rp-2017d14_en.pdf.

# Appendix E: Recent World Bank Research on Regional Integration in Africa

Recent research at the World Bank has shown that the African continent would benefit from deeper regional integration and offers useful background analysis for the proposed study. This appendix provides a brief summary.

## INTRAREGIONAL TRADE AND TRADE POLICY

The African Continental Free Trade Area (AfCFTA) could benefit from the lessons that emerged from the most recent World Bank study of trade policy and barriers in the Economic and Monetary Community of Central Africa (CEMAC)—see Fiess et al. (2018). The study finds that, despite significant regional integration efforts, trade within CEMAC remains limited for the following reasons. First, despite a common external tariff (CET), there is a significant divergence from CET at the national level. Second, CEMAC's average CET (18.1 percent) is higher when compared with those of other countries and other regions—for example, the CET of the Economic Community of West African States (ECOWAS) is 12.4 percent. The authors recommend converging to a tariff schedule with only four instead of five bands; eliminating the top tariff of 30 percent (which would simplify the tariff regime); lowering the average level of tariff protection; and reducing import prices. Third, the significant nontariff barriers and members' noncompliance with CEMAC transit agreements are preventing intraregional trade, particularly agricultural trade. Fourth, for regional integration to succeed, the broad political will for integration has to be consistent. The World Bank (2018) suggests deepening the common market by harmonizing customs exemptions; removing the remaining nontariff barriers; facilitating trade along trade corridors; implementing the CEMAC transit and customs regime; and setting and implementing regional standards for border agencies.

In studying the resource-rich countries in Sub-Saharan Africa (SSA), Izvorski, Coulibaly, and Doumbia (2018) find that although the region has established numerous integration arrangements, spillovers from the resource-rich countries to their neighbors have been negligible, including from Angola, Nigeria, and South Africa— the region's largest resource-rich middle-income countries. The essential pillar for rejuvenating growth in resource-rich SSA includes building up the institutions for regional integration, such as the establishment of the African Continental Free Trade Area. AfCFTA is expected to boost intraregional trade, strengthen the complementarities of production and exports, create employment, and limit the impact of commodity price volatility on the participants. The authors also suggest establishing preferential access for all countries in regional groupings to leading world markets with attractive rules of origin, conditional on their lead in promoting regional integration (Izvorski, Coulibaly, and Doumbia 2018).

## ESTIMATING THE IMPACT OF PREFERENTIAL TRADE AGREEMENTS IN AFRICA

The impacts of preferential trade agreements (PTAs) are thought to be heterogeneous for small developing countries, and the following studies evaluate the trade impacts and examine the determinants of these variations and the underlying mechanisms, which could be considered during the design of AfCFTA.

Coulibaly (2018) proposes a rigorous econometric strategy to reestimate the impact of the African Growth and Opportunity Act (AGOA) and the Everything But Arms (EBA) agreement from 2001 to 2015. The author finds that West Africa could be exporting 2.5 to 4 times more to the European Union and the United States if AGOA and EBA were not implemented in a differentiated manner in terms of country eligibility, product coverage,. and rules of origin. The author uses the Pseudo-Poisson Maximum Likelihood (PPML) gravity model estimation to properly account for the heteroscedasticity of bilateral trade flows as well zero trade flows.

Kassa and Coulibaly (2019) assess the impact of AGOA-eligible countries during the post-AGOA period, 2001–15, using the Synthetic Control Method (SCM), a quasi-experimental approach that estimates the gap between the synthetic counterfactual and the treatment, which represents the impact of the treatment after the treatment period. Kassa and Coulibaly (2019) find that most eligible countries registered gains in exports attributable to AGOA, although with varied results.

## INDUSTRY-SPECIFIC EMPIRICAL FINDINGS

In their industry-specific findings, Kassa and Coulibaly (2019) discover that most export gains stemmed from exports of petroleum and other minerals, whereas other countries saw gains in manufacturing and others in industrial goods. When the gains were derived from exports of fuel, they were uneven. When they were based on nonfuel exports, the gains were increasing over the years of AGOA eligibility.

The positive trade impacts are associated with improvements in information and communications technology (ICT) infrastructure, integrity in the institutions of legal and property rights, ease of labor market regulations, and a sound macroeconomic environment, including stable exchange rates and low inflation. Although undue exposure to either a single market such as the United States or a few commodities may have also restricted the gains from trade, the lesson for AfCFTA could be that, in the long term, its impact on exports could support the transformation of economies as long as measures are in place to support diversification of exports into nonfuel products such as manufacturing and agroprocessing.

According to Coulibaly (2018), the textile provision of AGOA has had a stronger positive impact on Sub-Saharan Africa exports to the United States than the general AGOA provision. For shorter time spans, the estimated effect of the textile provision of AGOA is even stronger: 75 percent more exports over 2001–03, 51 percent over 2004–06, and 88 percent over 2012–15, compared with 14 percent over 2001–15. The full set of simulations indicate that ECOWAS exports of nontextile products to the European Union or the United States could have been on average 2.5 times greater than the levels registered, and exports of textile products could have been four times greater.

## POLICY IMPLICATIONS FOR AN EFFECTIVE REGIONAL INTEGRATION IN AFRICA

Coulibaly (2018) concludes that given the estimated trade creation potential for a group of countries committed to deep regional integration, a revision of AGOA and EBA provisions to eliminate the differentiated eligibility criteria and rules of origin would make these PTAs a driving force behind the success of regional integration in Sub-Saharan Africa. Therefore, such potential for trade creation in a region coupled with revisions should be considered during the design process of AfCFTA.

The Kassa and Coulibaly (2019) study suggests that PTAs need to be reinforced using reform-based eligibility criteria. The authors recommend that during the design process of PTAs, countries should consider incorporating policy commitments along with preferential access across a range of areas to create an enabling environment for private investment and trade that could enhance export capacity. Lessons from AGOA might include efforts to ease supply constraints and support the integration of African economies into global trade by augmenting the quota- and tariff-free "preferential" agreements with additional instruments to strengthen the capacity and competitiveness of firms. Recent initiatives such as the Compact with Africa (CwA), with its strong focus on improving the business environment, building infrastructure, and promoting effective regulations and institutions, bridge preferential access with such policy frameworks. Expansion of quota- and tariff-free access to the products in which most African countries may have comparative advantage, such as agriculture and relevant manufacturing, may expand the benefits for African firms.

## REFERENCES

Coulibaly, Souleymane. 2018. "Differentiated Impact of AGOA and EBA on West African Countries." Office of the Chief Economist, Africa Region, World Bank, Washington, DC.

Fiess, Norbert Matthias, Philippe Marie Aguera, Cesar Calderon, Leif Jensen, Joanne Catherine Gaskell, John C. Keyser, Hannah Sibylle Nielsen, Alberto Portugal, and Jose E. Signoret. 2018. "Deepening Regional Integration to Advance Growth and Prosperity." World Bank Group, Washington, DC. http://documents.worldbank.org/curated/en/491781560455916201/Deepening -Regional-Integration-to-Advance-Growth-and-Prosperity.

Izvorski, Ivailo, Souleymane Coulibaly, and Djeneba Doumbia. 2018. *Reinvigorating Growth in Resource-Rich Sub-Saharan Africa*. Washington, DC: World Bank. https://doi.org/10.1596/30399.

Kassa, Woubet, and Souleymane Coulibaly. 2019. "Revisiting the Trade Impact of the African Growth and Opportunity Act: A Synthetic Control Approach." Working Paper 8993, World Bank, Washington, DC. https://doi.org/10.1596/1813-9450-8993.

# Appendix F: Data Sources

The key source of data for this analysis is the Global Trade Analysis Project (GTAP) database, coordinated by the Center for Global Trade Analysis in the Department of Agricultural Economics at Purdue University. This analysis uses a modified version of Version 10 prerelease 3.[1] The key modification compared with the official board release is the inclusion of the Democratic Republic of Congo as a separate country in the database using an input-output table provided by the World Bank. Angola is moved to the Central Africa regional aggregate. Three modifications of the standard GTAP database are introduced as changes to the reference data:

1. Introduction of observed statutory tariffs on traded goods and services imposed by African countries. These are provided by the World Bank
2. Incorporation of estimates of the quantification of nontariff barriers (NTBs) to traded goods based on estimates from Kee, Nicita, and Olarreaga (2009)
3. Incorporation of estimates of the quantification of barriers in the services trade based on estimates from Jafari and Tarr (2017).

These modifications are implemented using the Altertax procedure (Malcolm 1998). This procedure is intended to introduce modifications to the GTAP database that minimize distortions from the original database.

## NEW ESTIMATES OF STATUTORY TARIFFS

A database with import values from UN Comtrade and statutory tariffs from the Trade Analysis Information System (TRAINS) is constructed for 48 African countries for which data are available, and it is used for the simulations.[2] The database includes the most recent statutory data available for each country (see appendixes H and J).

Tariff lines are classified into one of three product categories (nonsensitive, sensitive, and excluded) to minimize tariff revenue losses. For this purpose, tariff lines for each country are ranked in descending order in terms of tariff revenues generated from imports in the African Continental Free Trade Area (AfCFTA). The bottom 90 percent of tariff lines are then classified as nonsensitive products, the next 7 percent of tariff lines as sensitive products, and the remaining 3 percent as excluded products. However, because of the limits agreed to on excluded products, the list of excluded products is revised to include only the tariff lines with the largest tariff revenues up to a cumulative intraregional import share of 10 percent, and the remaining tariff lines are reclassified as sensitive products. Because tariff revenues are more concentrated than imports, this results in exclusion lists with fewer than 10 percent of tariff lines for all countries.

## QUANTIFICATION OF NONTARIFF BARRIERS IN GOODS

Estimates of nontariff barriers for goods are taken from the World Bank's World Integrated Trade Solution (WITS) database, based on the methodology developed by Kee, Nicita, and Olarreaga (2009). The original data cover 78 developing and developed countries and goods at the Harmonized System 6 (HS6) level. In a first step, these estimates are converted to the 57-sector categories of the GTAP database.[3] The aggregated NTB database is in a CSV format (AVE_GTAP_Data.csv) with three fields: country International Organization for Standardization (ISO) code, GTAP sector code, and the value of the NTB estimates. The country coverage in Africa in this database is limited to Algeria (DZA), Burkina Faso (BFA), Cameroon (CMR), Côte d'Ivoire (CIV), the Arab Republic of Egypt (EGY), Ethiopia (ETH), Gabon (GAB), Ghana (GHA), Kenya (KEN), Madagascar (MDG), Malawi (MWI), Mali (MLI), Mauritius (MUS), Morocco (MAR), Nigeria (NGA), Rwanda (RWA), Senegal (SEN), South Africa (ZAF), Sudan (SDN), Tanzania (TZA), Tunisia (TUN), Uganda (UGA), and Zambia (ZMB). (A description of how the missing countries and sectors are treated appears later in this appendix.) The ad valorem equivalents (AVEs) are aggregated to the model level using GTAP's trade weights, defined as aggregate imports (across source regions) at border prices—that is, valued at c.i.f.—cost, insurance, and freight.[4]

Filling the gaps for the AVEs of goods is relatively straightforward. The average AVE over the countries is calculated using the estimates provided by Kee, Nicita, and Olarreaga (2009)—both the trade-weighted average and the simple average. After they are merged with the services NTBs, described shortly, the AVEs are converted so they have the correct labels and are saved in a GDX for use as inputs to the Altertax procedure. The latter defaults to using the unweighted (the simple average of) the AVEs.[5]

## QUANTIFICATION OF NONTARIFF BARRIERS IN SERVICES

Estimates of services trade barriers are sourced from Jafari and Tarr (2017). The services covered in Jafari and Tarr (2017) only loosely line up with the GTAP services classification. Table F.1 shows the services classification in their study and the estimates of the services trade barriers for selected regions.

The Jafari and Tarr (2017) data were obtained as 11 separate Excel files (with macros)—one for each of their sectors. The data were collated into a single database

Table F.1    AVEs of Jafari and Tarr service sectors

|  | North Africa (NAF) | Sub-Saharan Africa (SSA) | Rest of East Asia | Western Europe | Rest of the world |
|---|---|---|---|---|---|
| Accounting | 54 | 31 | 43 | 28 | 32 |
| Legal | 60 | 45 | 63 | 28 | 41 |
| Air | 55 | 23 | 46 | 16 | 38 |
| Rail | 59 | 59 | 57 | 18 | 50 |
| Road | 36 | 31 | 45 | 24 | 33 |
| Banking | 17 | 15 | 17 | 2 | 16 |
| Insurance | 29 | 31 | 26 | 11 | 26 |
| Fixed line | 13 | 546 | 134 | 4 | 75 |
| Mobile | 1 | 3 | 1 | 1 | 1 |
| Retail | 5 | 2 | 4 | 1 | 3 |
| Maritime | 67 | 12 | 40 | 7 | 30 |

*Source:* Jafari and Tarr 2017, table 2.4.

*Note:* AVE = ad valorem equivalent.

in an Excel file (the "Data" worksheet in ServicesAVE.xlsx) with the country names replaced by their corresponding ISO codes. The country coverage for Africa consists of Algeria (DZA), Botswana (BWA), Burundi (BDI), Cameroon (CMR), Côte d'Ivoire (CIV), the Democratic Republic of Congo (COD), the Arab Republic of Egypt (EGY), Ethiopia (ETH), Ghana (GHA), Kenya (KEN), Lesotho (LSO), Madagascar (MDG), Malawi (MWI), Mali (MLI), Mauritius (MUS), Morocco (MAR), Mozambique (MOZ), Namibia (NAM), Nigeria (NGA), Rwanda (RWA), Senegal (SEN), South Africa (ZAF), Tanzania (TZA), Tunisia (TUN), Uganda (UGA), Zambia (ZMB), and Zimbabwe (ZWE). Table F.1 displays the simple averages for each of the 11 service sectors for two African regions and for the remaining non-Africa aggregate regions.

A second step maps the modeled countries and regions to the data from Jafari and Tarr (2017) or one of the aggregate regions in table F.1. The missing data include rest of North Africa (XNF), which is mapped to North Africa (NAF) as shown in table F.1. Benin, Burkina Faso, Guinea, Togo, rest of West Africa, rest of Central Africa (XCF), rest of South-Central Africa (XAC), rest of East Africa (XEC), and rest of SACU (South African Customs Union) are all mapped to the Sub-Saharan (SSA) column in table F.1. All other countries are mapped to their corresponding data in the AVE estimates of Jafari and Tarr (2017). This step is essentially carried out in the "ServicesAVE.xlsx" spreadsheet, and the resulting table (with the range name of SRVAVE in the "Agg" worksheet) is read by the GAMS aggregation routine for additional processing.

A third step maps the Jafari and Tarr (2017) sectors to the corresponding service sectors used in the model. Table F.2 shows the mapping and the weights. For example,

**Table F.2**  Mapping of Jafari and Tarr service sectors with model's service sectors

|  | Model | Weight |
|---|---|---|
| Accounting | obs | 0.5 |
| Legal | obs | 0.5 |
| Air | atp | 1.0 |
| Rail | otp | 0.5 |
| Road | otp | 0.5 |
| Banking | ofi | 1.0 |
| Insurance | isr | 1.0 |
| Fixed line | cmn | 0.1 |
| Mobile | cmn | 0.9 |
| Retail | trd | 1.0 |
| Maritime | wtp | 1.0 |

*Source:* World Bank study team.

*Note:* obs = other business services; atp = air transport; cmn = communication; isr = insurance; ofi = financial services not elsewhere classified (nec); otp = transport nec; trd = trade; wtp = water transport.

the AVE in the model's "other business services" (OBS) is mapped to accounting and legal services—each with a weight of 0.5.

## QUANTIFICATION OF TRADE FACILITATION MEASURES

Following the signing of the trade facilitation agreement (TFA) in December 2013, the Organisation for Economic Co-operation and Development (OECD) produced a series of 11 trade facilitation indicators (identified from A to K) for monitoring the TFA targets. Data for these indicators are available for 43 African countries. Each indicator takes a value of between 0 (no implementation) and 2 (full implementation). This analysis uses the estimates of de Melo and Sorgho (2019), who apply a model that predicts observed time in customs as a function of basic structural variables (GDP, Logistics Performance Index, and Infrastructure Quality Index); policy variables (World Governance Indicators); and the trade facilitation variables captured by the trade facilitation indicator (row L). Row L is a weighted average of the following components: (1) information availability; (2) involvement of the trade community; (3) advance rulings; (4) appeal procedures; (5) fees and charges; (6) formalities involving documents; (7) formalities involving automation; (8) formalities involving procedures; (9) internal border agency cooperation; (10) external border agency cooperation; and (11) governance and impartiality.

The model shows, after controlling for the structural and policy variables, that a higher trade facilitation indicator score reduces the probability of a longer time in customs. The overall differences in reductions in costs reflect disparities in trade facilitation indicator values and in time in customs for imports. The model provides estimates of the time reductions in customs as a result of full implementation of the TFA. Those reductions are then translated into ad valorem equivalents of barriers using the methodology of Hummels and Schaur (2012), who estimate that one extra day in customs is equivalent to a 1.3 percent extra tariff at the destination based on maritime trade flows to the United States.

To simulate the gains from implementing the TFA, the analysis applies the econometric estimates of the AVEs of time lost in customs by a regional economic community (REC). The estimates for the 47 individual countries are used to build up the averages at the REC level. The AVE estimates in the model are for 21 countries. For the aggregate regions, the analysis applies the average for the corresponding group to which they belong—that is, XNF is mapped to the Algerian estimate; XAC is mapped to the estimate for Angola; XEC is mapped to the average estimate for Burundi, Comoros, and Sudan; XCF is mapped to the average estimate for Chad, the Democratic Republic of Congo, and Gabon; and XWF is mapped to the average estimate for Liberia, Mali, Niger, and Sierra Leone. For the missing estimates, Côte d'Ivoire and Guinea are mapped to the estimate for the XWF region, and Botswana, Mauritius, Namibia, and the rest of SACU (XSC) are mapped to the estimate for South Africa. In the simulations, it is assumed that improvements apply to imports that are likely to arrive in 20-foot (or 40-foot) containers, which means excluding imports of mining products, fossil fuels, and refined oil.

## NOTES

1. GTAP prereleases are available only to GTAP Consortium members.
2. No recent data were available for six countries: Equatorial Guinea, Eritrea, Libya, Somalia, South Sudan, and Sudan.
3. Thanks to Jean-Marc Solleder for the aggregation. The prerelease 3 and final release of Version 10 of the GTAP database have 65 sectors. The 57-sector estimates were converted to the new 65-sector scheme assuming uniformity across the new subgroups. An improvement would consist of reaggregating the HS6 level estimates to the new 65-sector GTAP classification.
4. The read-in 57-sector country-level estimates are stored in the parameter AVEC0, which is converted to the 65-sector level and stored as AVEC. The country-level estimates are converted to the GTAP region-level estimates (at the 65-sector level) and stored in AVER. The final step aggregates the GTAP-level regions and sectors to the model's regions and sectors using trade weights, which produces the parameter AVE. No regional aggregation is involved here because there is largely a one-to-one mapping between the country-level AVE estimates and the country coverage in GTAP—that is, none of the countries in the estimates by Kee, Nicita, and Olarreaga (2009) is part of a GTAP regional aggregation. There are, however, three exceptions: the XEF region is composed of Iceland (from the Kee, Nicita, and Olarreaga 2009 estimates); the XWS is composed of Lebanon; and the XNF region is composed of Algeria.
5. The parameter AVE is converted to the parameter AVE0 and AVE_WGT0. Both use AVE for all countries in the original Kee, Nicita, and Olarreaga (2009) database for goods and services AVEs. For the missing countries and regions, the simple and weighted averages are merged. The labels of these parameters are then converted and stored in a GDX file for Altertax.

## REFERENCES

de Melo, J., and Z. Sorgho. 2019. "The Landscape of Rules of Origin across African RECs in a Comparative Perspectives with Suggestions for Harmonization." Fondation pour Les Études et Recherches sur le Développement International, Clermont-Ferrand, France.

Hummels, David, and Georg Schaur. 2012. "Time as a Trade Barrier." NBER working paper, National Bureau of Economic Research, Cambridge, MA.

Jafari, Yaghoob, and David G. Tarr. 2017. "Estimates of Ad Valorem Equivalents of Barriers against Foreign Suppliers of Services in Eleven Services Sectors and 103 Countries." *World Economy* 40 (3): 544–73. https://doi.org/10.1111/twec.12329.

Kee, Hiau Looi, Alessandro Nicita, and Marcelo Olarreaga. 2009. "Estimating Trade Restrictiveness Indices." *Economic Journal* 119 (534): 172–99. https://doi.org/10.1111/j.1468-0297.2008.02209.x.

Malcolm, G. 1998. "Modeling Country Risks and Capital Flows in GTAP." GTAP Technical Paper 13. Center for Global Trade Analysis, Purdue University, West Lafayette, IN. https://www.gtap.agecon .purdue.edu/resources/res_display.asp?RecordID=316.

# Appendix G: Summary Description of the ENVISAGE Model

The Environmental Impact and Sustainability Applied General Equilibrium (ENVISAGE) model follows the circular flow of an economy paradigm. Firms purchase input factors (such as labor and capital) to produce goods and services. Households receive factor income and in turn demand the goods and services produced by firms. Equality of supply and demand determine the equilibrium prices for factors, goods, and services. The model is solved as a sequence of comparative static equilibria in which the factors of production are exogenous for each time period and linked between time periods with accumulation expressions. Production is implemented as a series of nested constant-elasticity-of-substitution (CES) functions aimed at capturing the substitutability across all inputs. Three production archetypes are implemented: (1) for crops, reflecting the intensification of inputs versus land intensification; (2) for livestock, reflecting range-fed versus ranch-fed production; and (3) as the default, revolving largely around capital/labor substitutability. Some production activities highlight specific inputs (for example, agricultural chemicals in crops and feed in livestock), and all activities include energy and its components as part of the cost minimization paradigm. Production is also identified by vintage—divided into *old* and *new*—with typically lower substitution possibilities associated with *old* capital.

Each production activity is allowed to produce more than one commodity—for example, the ethanol sector can produce ethanol and distiller's dried grains with solubles (DDGS). And commodities can be formed by the output of one or more activities (such as electricity). ENVISAGE therefore uses a different classification of activities and commodities.[1] One of the features of the model is that it integrates the new Global Trade Analysis Project (GTAP) power database that disaggregates GTAP's electricity sector ("ely") into 11 different power sources plus electricity transmission and distribution. Although the database has both a supply and a demand side for all 11 power sources, the aggregation facility permits aggregation of electricity demand into a single commodity and the "make" matrix specification combines the output from the different power activities into a single electricity commodity.

Income accrues from payments to factors of production and is allocated to households (after taxes). The government sector accrues all net tax payments and purchases goods and services. The model incorporates multiple utility functions for determining household demand. A set of three household demand functions is linked to the ubiquitous linear expenditure system (LES): (1) the standard LES; (2) the extended LES (ELES) that incorporates household saving into the utility function; and (3) an implicitly directly additive demand system (AIDADS) that allows for nonlinear Engel curves in the LES framework.[2] The fourth option relies on the constant differences in elasticity (CDE) utility function that is used in the core GTAP model (Corong et al. 2017; Hertel 1997). The ELES framework incorporates the decision to save in a top-level utility function. The other demand systems assume savings is an exogenous proportion of disposable income in the default closure. The consumer utility function determines consumer demand bundles that are subsequently converted to produced goods using a consumer demand "make" or transition matrix. Investment is savings driven and equal to domestic savings adjusted by net capital flows.

Trade is modeled using the so-called Armington specification, which posits that the demand for goods is differentiated by region of origin. The model allows for domestic/import sourcing at the aggregate level (after aggregating domestic absorption across all agents) or at the agent level. In the standard specification, a second Armington nest allocates aggregate import demand across all exporting regions using a representative agent specification.

A newer though minimally tested version of the model known as the MRIO specification allows for sourcing imports by agent. Exports are modeled in an analogous fashion using a nested constant-elasticity-of-transformation (CET) specification. The domestic supply of each commodity is passed to the domestic market and an aggregate export bundle using a top-level CET function. The latter is allocated across regions of destination using a second-level CET function.[3] Each bilateral trade node is associated with four prices: (1) producer price; (2) export border price, also referred to as the free on board (FOB) price; (3) import border price, also known as the cost, insurance, and freight (CIF) price; and (4) the end-user price, which includes all applicable trade taxes. The wedge between the producer price and the FOB price repesents the export tax (or subsidy if negative), and the wedge between the CIF and end-user prices represents the import tariff (and perhaps other import-related distortions). Finally, the wedge between the CIF and FOB prices represents the international trade and transport margins. These margins represent in turn the use of the real resources supplied by each region. The global international trade and transport sector purchases these services from each region in order to minimize the aggregate cost.

The model has two fundamental markets for goods and services: (1) domestically produced goods sold on the domestic market and (2) domestically produced goods sold by region of destination. All other goods and services are composite bundles of these goods. Two market equilibrium conditions are needed to clear these two markets.[4]

The model incorporates five types of production factors: (1) labor (up to five types); (2) capital; (3) land; (4) a sector-specific natural resource (such as fossil fuel energy reserves); and (5) water. Segmentation of the labor market is allowed (though

**Figure G.1**    Structure of value added in the production function

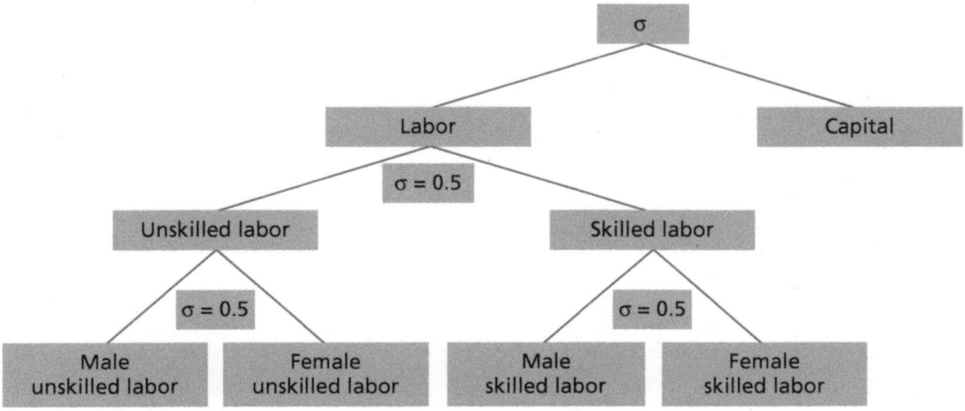

*Source:* Calculations based on customs and statutory data, World Bank study team.

not required)—typically agriculture versus nonagriculture. The model also allows for regime switching between full and partial wage flexibility. In this gender-sensitive version of the model, the labor bundle is composed of four labor types—skilled and unskilled labor, each broken out by gender (figure G.1). At a first stage, the aggregate labor bundle is composed of skilled and unskilled labor. In the default parameterization, the substitution elasticity is 0.5. Each skill bundle, unskilled and skilled, is composed of labor by gender—male and female. The default substitution elasticity is 0.5 across gender. This implies that all four labor types are equally substitutable in the default configuration.

Capital is allocated across sectors to equalize rates of return. If all sectors are expanding, *old* capital is assumed to receive the economywide rate of return. In contracting sectors, *old* capital is sold on secondary markets using an upward sloping supply curve. This implies that capital is only partially mobile across sectors. Aggregate land and water supply are specified using supply curves. Although there are several options, the preferred supply curve is a logistic function that has an upper bound. Water demand also includes exogenous components for environmental uses and groundwater recharge. Land and water are allocated across activities using a nested CET specification.[5] Natural resources are supplied to each sector using an isoelastic supply function, with the possibility of differentiated elasticities, depending on market conditions.

ENVISAGE incorporates the main greenhouse gases—carbon, methane, nitrous oxides, and fluorinated gases. It also incorporates 10 nongreenhouse gases[6] that may have impacts on the atmosphere and climate change, and yet often also have significant local impacts, particularly on health. Emissions are generated by consumption of commodities (such as fuels) and factor use (such as land in rice production and herds in livestock production). There are also processed base emissions such as methane from landfills.[7]

A number of carbon control regimes are available in the model. Carbon taxes can be imposed exogenously—potentially differentiated across regions. The incidence of the carbon tax allows partial or full exemption by commodity and end user. For example, households can be exempted from the carbon tax on natural gas consumption. The model allows emission caps in a flexible manner—regions can be segmented into coalitions on a multiregional or global basis. In addition to the standard cap system, a cap and trade system can be defined in which each region within a coalition is assigned an initial emission quota.

Dynamics involves three elements: labor supply, capital stock, and technological change. Labor supply (by skill level) grows at an exogenously determined rate. The aggregate capital supply evolves according to the standard stock/flow motion equation—that is, the capital stock at the beginning of each period is equal to the previous period's capital stock less depreciation plus the previous period's level of investment. Finally, the standard version of the model assumes that labor augments technological change calibrated to given assumptions about growth of the gross domestic product (GDP) and intersectoral productivity differences. In policy simulations, technology is typically assumed to be fixed at the calibrated levels.

For this particular analysis, the key model specifications include:

- An agent-based Armington specification for import demand with an aggregate agent allocation of total import demand by source region
- Capture of the value of time in trade by an iceberg parameter specified for each commodity and bilateral trade node. The iceberg parameter is assumed to be fixed over time in the baseline. The model has a separate iceberg parameter for imports and exports.
- Diagonal make matrix—that is, one-to-one correspondence between activities and commodities
- Constant differences in elasticity utility function
- Logistic aggregate land supply function
- Fixed capital account within each time period at reference year levels, implying that the capital acccount declines over time as a share of GDP.

The model's reference year is 2014, and it is initialized and calibrated to the GTAP database, Version 10 prerelease 3.[8] The 141 regions in the database were aggregated to 34 regions (table G.1). Similarly, the database's 65 sectors were aggregated to 21 sectors (table G.2), with an emphasis on the more traded manufacturing sectors and the trade and transport services.

The key macroeconomic drivers of the baseline rely on a number of existing baselines. Population growth is calibrated to the United Nations Population Division's 2015 projection, the medium variant.[9] The baseline GDP is calibrated to Shared Socio-Economic Pathway 2 (SSP2). The five SSPs were developed by the Integrated Assessment Modeling (IAM) community to provide a macroeconomic framework for quantitative

Table G.1   Regional dimension

| Region name (code) | |
| --- | --- |
| 1 | Egypt, Arab Rep. (EGY) |
| 2 | Morocco (MAR) |
| 3 | Tunisia (TUN) |
| 4 | Rest of North Africa (XNF) |
| 5 | Burkina Faso (BFA) |
| 6 | Cameroon (CMR) |
| 7 | Côte d'Ivoire (CIV) |
| 8 | Ghana (GHA) |
| 9 | Nigeria (NGA) |
| 10 | Senegal (SEN) |
| 11 | Rest of West Africa (XWF) |
| 12 | Central Africa (XCF) |
| 13 | Congo, Dem. Rep. (COD) |
| 14 | Ethiopia (ETH) |
| 15 | Kenya (KEN) |
| 16 | Madagascar (MDG) |
| 17 | Malawi (MWI) |
| 18 | Mauritius (MUS) |
| 19 | Mozambique (MOZ) |
| 20 | Rwanda (RWA) |
| 21 | Tanzania (TZA) |
| 22 | Uganda (UGA) |
| 23 | Zambia (ZMB) |
| 24 | Zimbabwe (ZWE) |
| 25 | Rest of East Africa (XEC) |
| 26 | Botswana (BWA) |
| 27 | Namibia (NAM) |
| 28 | South Africa (ZAF) |
| 29 | Rest of South African Customs Union (XSC) |
| 30 | China (CHN) |
| 31 | Rest of East Asia (XEA) |
| 32 | United States (USA) |
| 33 | European Union + EFTA (weu) |
| 34 | Rest of the world (row) |

*Note:* EFTA = European Free Trade Association.

**Table G.2**   Sector dimension

| Sector name (code) | |
|---|---|
| 1 | Agriculture (AGR) |
| 2 | Fossil fuels (FFL) |
| 3 | Minerals, NES (OXT) |
| 4 | Processed foods (PFD) |
| 5 | Wood and paper products (WPP) |
| 6 | Textiles and wearing apparel (TWP) |
| 7 | Energy-intensive manufacturing (KE5) |
| 8 | Petroleum and coal products (P_C) |
| 9 | Chemical, rubber, and plastic products (crp) |
| 10 | Manufactures, NES (XMN) |
| 11 | Construction (CNS) |
| 12 | Trade services (TRD) |
| 13 | Road and rail transport services (OTP) |
| 14 | Water transport services (WTP) |
| 15 | Air transport services (ATP) |
| 16 | Communications services (CMN) |
| 17 | Other financial services (OFI) |
| 18 | Insurance and real estate services (INS) |
| 19 | Other business services (OBS) |
| 20 | Recreational and other services (ROS) |
| 21 | Public services (XSV) |

*Note:* NES = not elsewhere specified.

analysis of the economics of climate change.[10] Three economic modeling groups have quantified global GDP projections: the Organisation for Economic Co-operation and Development (OECD), International Institute for Applied Systems Analysis (IIASA), and Potsdam Institute for Climate Impact Research (PIK). All three teams harmonized to the same demographic projections provided by IIASA's demographic unit. This analysis uses the OECD-based SSP2 projection. SSP2—called the middle of the road scenario—is treated by many modeling groups as a business-as-usual scenario.

Labor force growth is being generated by the GIDD projections (appendix A). The projections are available by broad age group (the 15–64 age cohort for the labor force is used here), gender, and education (primary, secondary, and tertiary). The growth of skilled labor is equated with the growth of specific education categories. For low- and lower-middle-income countries, skilled workers are equated with the secondary and tertiary level. For upper-middle and high-income countries, skilled workers are equated only with the tertiary level. The baseline scenario tracks the per capita income growth of countries and implements a switch in the definition of skilled workers if a country graduates from lower-middle-income status to upper-middle-income status (using the 2014 World Bank income thresholds).[11]

The analysis targets real GDP growth by calibrating labor productivity in the baseline. It allows for sector differences in labor productivity growth, with a (fixed) higher rate in agriculture and manufacturing relative to services. Other factors that affect calibrated labor productivity include an exogenous improvement in energy efficiency, agricultural yields, and international trade and transport margins.

The baseline also incorporates the following exogenous assumptions:

- The income parameter of the CDE is adjusted between periods based on an estimated economic relation between the income parameter and aggregate per capita consumption. The parameterization of the relationship is based on a least-squares estimate using the base year GTAP database. One key purpose is to reduce the share of food expenditures as incomes rise.
- Capital accumulation is based on the standard capital motion equation $Kt = (1 - 8)Kt - 1 + It - 1$. Thus the capital stock trends depend on investment and savings decisions. In the baseline, household savings are adjusted in order to target future trends in the investment to GDP ratio, with the basic idea that these trends should more or less line up with steady state returns to capital.

The following is a brief outline of the contours of the baseline for this analysis:[12]

- World population is expected to rise from 7.3 billion in 2014 to 8.8 billion in 2035, an increase of around 1.5 billion with a annual growth rate of about 1 percent on average.
- Population growth in Africa accounts for 45 percent of the increase, with an increase of 700 million, some 61 percent from the 2014 base of 1.1 billion. This figure translates into a blistering annual growth rate of 2.3 percent, compared with 0.6 percent for the rest of the world. Africa's share of the global population increases from 16 percent to 21 percent.
- Global GDP will rise from US$82 trillion in 2014 to US$158 trillion in 2035— an average annual increase of 3.2 percent.
- The annual growth rate of GDP in Africa is a relatively rapid 5.8 percent between 2014 and 2035, somewhat tempered by high population growth. Nevertheless, Africa sees its share of global output increase from 3.7 percent to 6.2 percent (at constant 2014 U.S. dollar prices and market exchange rates).

- Average per capita income in Africa rises from US$2,600 to US$5,300 between 2014 and 2035, growing at an annual clip of 3.4 percent. The global average income rises from US$11,300 to US$19,700 over the same period—an annual growth rate of 2.2 percent.
- African incomes exhibit some convergence to the world average, with the parity index rising from 23 percent to 30 percent.

Tables G.3 and G.4 provide the GTAP regional and sectoral concordance, respectively, used in this analysis.

**Table G.3**   GTAP regional concordance

|    | Region | GTAP concordance |
|----|--------|------------------|
| 1  | Egypt, Arab Rep. (EGY) | Egypt, Arab Rep. (EGY) |
| 2  | Morocco (MAR) | Morocco (MAR) |
| 3  | Tunisia (TUN) | Tunisia (TUN) |
| 4  | Rest of North Africa (XNF) | Rest of North Africa (XNF) |
| 5  | Burkina Faso (BFA) | Burkina Faso (BFA) |
| 6  | Cameroon (CMR) | Cameroon (CMR) |
| 7  | Côte d'Ivoire (CIV) | Côte d'Ivoire (CIV) |
| 8  | Ghana (GHA) | Ghana (GHA) |
| 9  | Nigeria (NGA) | Nigeria (NGA) |
| 10 | Senegal (SEN) | Senegal (SEN) |
| 11 | Rest of West Africa (XWF) | Benin (BEN), Guinea (GIN), Togo (TGO), Rest of West Africa (XWF) |
| 12 | Central Africa (XCF) | Central Africa (XCF) |
| 13 | Congo, Dem. Rep. (COD) | Congo, Dem. Rep. (COD) |
| 14 | Ethiopia (ETH) | Ethiopia (ETH) |
| 15 | Kenya (KEN) | Kenya (KEN) |
| 16 | Madagascar (MDG) | Madagascar (MDG) |
| 17 | Malawi (MWI) | Malawi (MWI) |
| 18 | Mauritius (MUS) | Mauritius (MUS) |
| 19 | Mozambique (MOZ) | Mozambique (MOZ) |
| 20 | Rwanda (RWA) | Rwanda (RWA) |
| 21 | Tanzania (TZA) | Tanzania (TZA) |

*continued*

**Table G.3**   GTAP regional concordance (*continued*)

| | Region | GTAP concordance |
|---|---|---|
| 22 | Uganda (UGA) | Uganda (UGA) |
| 23 | Zambia (ZMB) | Zambia (ZMB) |
| 24 | Zimbabwe (ZWE) | Zimbabwe (ZWE) |
| 25 | Rest of East Africa (XEC) | Rest of East Africa (XEC) |
| 26 | Botswana (BWA) | Botswana (BWA) |
| 27 | Namibia (NAM) | Namibia (NAM) |
| 28 | South Africa (ZAF) | South Africa (ZAF) |
| 29 | Rest of South African Customs Union (XSC) | Rest of South African Customs Union (XSC) |
| 30 | China (CHN) | China (CHN) |
| 31 | Rest of East Asia (XEA) | Hong Kong, SAR, China (HKG), Japan (JPN), Mongolia (MNG), Republic of Korea (KOR), Taiwan, China (TWN), rest of East Asia (XEA), Brunei Darussalam (BRN), Cambodia (KHM), Indonesia (IDN), Lao PDR (LAO), Malaysia (MYS), Philippines (PHL), Singapore (SGP), Thailand (THA), Vietnam (VNM), rest of Southeast Asia (XSE) |
| 32 | United States (USA) | United States of America (USA) |
| 33 | European Union + EFTA (weu) | Austria (AUT), Belgium (BEL), Cyprus (CYP), Czech Republic (CZE), Denmark (DNK), Estonia (EST), Finland (FIN), France (FRA), Germany (DEU), Greece (GRC), Hungary (HUN), Ireland (IRL), Italy (ITA), Latvia (LVA), Lithuania (LTU), Luxembourg (LUX), Malta (MLT), Netherlands (NLD), Poland (POL), Portugal (PRT), Slovakia (SVK), Slovenia (SVN), Spain (ESP), Sweden (SWE), United Kingdom (GBR), Switzerland (CHE), Norway (NOR), rest of EFTA (XEF), Bulgaria (BGR), Croatia (HRV), Romania (ROU) |
| 34 | Rest of the world (row) | Australia (AUS), New Zealand (NZL), rest of Oceania (XOC), Bangladesh (BGD), India (IND), Nepal (NPL), Pakistan (PAK), Sri Lanka (LKA), rest of South Asia (XSA), Canada (CAN), Mexico (MEX), rest of North America (XNA), Argentina (ARG), Bolivia (BOL), Brazil (BRA), Chile (CHL), Colombia (COL), Ecuador (ECU), Paraguay (PRY), Peru (PER), Uruguay (URY), Venezuela (VEN), rest of South America (XSM), Costa Rica (CRI), Guatemala (GTM), Honduras (HND), Nicaragua (NIC), Panama (PAN), El Salvador (SLV), rest of Central America (XCA), Dominican Republic (DOM), Jamaica (JAM), Puerto Rico (PRI), Trinidad and Tobago (TTO), rest of Caribbean (XCB), Albania (ALB), Belarus (BLR), Russian Federation (RUS), Ukraine (UKR), rest of East Europe (XEE), rest of Europe (XER), Kazakhstan (KAZ), Kyrgyzstan (KGZ), Tajikistan (TJK), rest of former Soviet Union (XSU), Armenia (ARM), Azerbaijan (AZE), Georgia (GEO), Bahrain (BHR), Iran, Islamic Rep. (IRN), Israel (ISR), Jordan (JOR), Kuwait (KWT), Oman (OMN), Qatar (QAT), Saudi Arabia (SAU), Turkey (TUR), United Arab Emirates (ARE), rest of Western Asia (XWS), rest of the world (XTW) |

*Note:* EFTA = European Free Trade Association; GTAP = Global Trade Analysis Project.

**Table G.4**  GTAP sector concordance

| | Sector name | GTAP concordance |
|---|---|---|
| 1 | Agriculture (AGR) | Paddy rice (PDR); wheat (WHT); cereal grains, NEC (GRO); vegetables, fruit, nuts (V_F); oilseeds (OSD); sugar cane, sugar beet (C_B); plant-based fibers (PFB); crops, NEC (OCR); bovine cattle, sheep and goats, horses (CTL); animal products, NEC (OAP); raw milk (RMK); wool, silkworm cocoons (WOL); forestry (FRS) |
| 2 | Fossil fuels (FFL) | Coal (COA); oil (OIL); gas (GAS), gas manufacture, distribution (GDT) |
| 3 | Minerals, NES (OXT) | Other extraction (formerly other manufacturing (omn) minerals, NEC) (OXT) |
| 4 | Processed foods (PFD) | Fish (FSH); bovine meat products (CMT); meat products, NEC (OMT); vegetable oils and fats (VOL); dairy products (MIL); processed rice (PCR); sugar (SGR); food products, NEC (OFD); beverages and tobacco products (B_T) |
| 5 | Wood and paper products (WPP) | Wood products (LUM); paper products, publishing (PPP) |
| 6 | Textiles and wearing apparel (TWP) | Textiles (TEX); wearing apparel (WAP); leather products (LEA) |
| 7 | Energy-intensive manufacturing (KE5) | Mineral products, NEC (NMM); ferrous metals (I_S); metals, NEC (NFM) |
| 8 | Petroleum and coal products (P_C) | Petroleum, coal products (P_C) |
| 9 | Chemical, rubber, and plastic products (CRP) | Chemical products (CHM); basic pharmaceutical products (BPH); rubber and plastic products (RPP) |
| 10 | Manufactures, NES (XMN) | Metal products (FMP); computer, electronic, and optical products (ELE); electrical equipment (EEQ); machinery and equipment, NEC (OME); motor vehicles and parts (MVH); transport equipment, NEC (OTN); manufactures, NEC (OMF) |
| 11 | Construction (CNS) | Construction (CNS) |
| 12 | Trade services (TRD) | Trade (TRD); accommodation, food, and service activities (AFS); warehousing and support activities (WHS) |
| 13 | Road and rail transport services (OTP) | Transport, NEC (OTP) |
| 14 | Water transport services (WTP) | Water transport (WTP) |
| 15 | Air transport services (ATP) | Air transport (ATP) |
| 16 | Communications services (CMN) | Communication (CMN) |
| 17 | Other financial services (OFI) | Financial services, NEC (OFI) |
| 18 | Insurance and real estate services (INS) | Insurance (formerly ISR) (INS) |
| 19 | Other business services (OBS) | Real estate activities (RSA); business services, NEC (OBS) |
| 20 | Public services (XSV) | Electricity (ELY); water (WTR); public administration and defense (OSG); education (EDU); human health and social work activities (HHT); dwellings (DWE) |

*Note:* NEC = not elsewhere classified; NES = not elsewhere specified.

## NOTES

1. Production activities are indexed with *a* and commodities are indexed with *i*.

2. Users can also specify implementing a Cobb-Douglas (CD) utility function, which can be considered part of the LES framework.

3. The model allows for perfect transformation, which is the standard specification in the GTAP model.

4. If there are $N$ commodities and $R$ regions, there will be $R \times N$ market clearing conditions for domestic goods and $R \times N \times R$ market clearing conditions for bilateral trade.

5. Land is implemented only for agricultural activities. Water demand by activity is present only in irrigated crop sectors. Other water demand is based on aggregate demand functions with market clearing, but it is not part of the cost structure.

6. Black carbon (BC), carbon monoxide (CO), ammonia ($NH_3$), volatile organic compounds (VOCs—NMVB and NMVF), nitrogen oxides ($NO_x$), organic carbon (OC), particulate matter ($PM_{10}$ and $PM_{2.5}$), and sulfur dioxide ($SO_2$).

7. The current version of the model does not include carbon emissions from deforestation—an important source of global carbon emissions.

8. Prereleases are made available only to GTAP Consortium members. The public version of Version 10 was posted on July 31, 2019. The database used for this analysis is a special version of Version 10 prelease 3; it includes the Democratic Republic of Congo (COD) as a separate region using an input-output table provided by the World Bank. Angola was aggregated with the Central Africa region. COD is not yet available in other versions of the database.

9. http://www.un.org/en/development/desa/publications/world-population-prospects-2015 -revision.html.

10. A special issue of *Global Environmental Change* provides significant background material on the SSPs and their development. See, in particular, Dellink et al. (2017) for a discussion of the OECD-based macroeconomic drivers.

11. The respective thresholds for 2014 are US$1,045, US$4,125, and US$12,736.

12. Additional details and tables are available from the World Bank study team.

## REFERENCES

Corong, Erwin L., Thomas W. Hertel, Robert A. Mcdougall, Marinos E. Tsigas, and Dominique van der Mensbrugghe. 2017. "The Standard GTAP Model, Version 7." *Journal of Global Economic Analysis* 2 (1): 1–119. https://jgea.org/resources/jgea/ojs/index.php/jgea/article/view/47.

Dellink, R., J. Chateau, E. Lanzi, and B. Magné. 2017. "Long-Term Economic Growth Projections in the Shared Socioeconomic Pathways." *Global Environmental Change* 42: 200–14. https://doi .org/10.1016/J.GLOENVCHA.2015.06.004.

Hertel, Thomas. 1997. "Global Trade Analysis: Modeling and Applications." Center for Global Trade Analysis, Department of Agricultural Economics, Purdue University. https://EconPapers.repec.org /RePEc:gta:gtapbk:7685.

# Appendix H: Statutory Tariff Data Availability by Country

**Table H.1** Availability of tariff data by country

| ISO 3166 | Country | Imports | Tariff |
|----------|---------|---------|--------|
| AGO | Angola | 2015 | 2016 |
| BDI | Burundi | 2017 | 2016 |
| BEN | Benin | 2016 | 2016 |
| BFA | Burkina Faso | 2016 | 2016 |
| BWA | Botswana | 2017 | 2016 |
| CAF | Central African Republic | 2016 | 2016 |
| CIV | Côte d'Ivoire | 2015 | 2016 |
| CMR | Cameroon | 2017 | 2014 |
| COG | Congo, Rep. | 2017 | 2015 |
| COM | Comoros | 2017 | 2015 |
| CPV | Cabo Verde | 2017 | 2015 |
| DJI | Djibouti | 2017 | 2014 |
| DZA | Algeria | 2017 | 2016 |
| EGY | Egypt, Arab Rep. | 2017 | 2016 |
| ERI | Eritrea | — | — |
| ETH | Ethiopia | 2015 | 2015 |
| GAB | Gabon | 2017 | 2016 |
| GHA | Ghana | 2017 | 2016 |
| GIN | Guinea | 2015 | 2012 |
| GMB | Gambia, The | 2016 | 2013 |
| GNB | Guinea-Bissau | 2017 | 2014 |
| GNQ | Equatorial Guinea | — | — |

*continued*

**Table H.1**    Availability of tariff data by country (*continued*)

| ISO 3166 | Country | Imports | Tariff |
|----------|---------|---------|--------|
| KEN | Kenya | 2017 | 2016 |
| LBR | Liberia | 2017 | 2014 |
| LBY | Libya | — | — |
| LSO | Lesotho | 2017 | 2016 |
| MAR | Morocco | 2016 | 2016 |
| MDG | Madagascar | 2017 | 2016 |
| MLI | Mali | 2017 | 2016 |
| MOZ | Mozambique | 2016 | 2016 |
| MRT | Mauritania | 2017 | 2015 |
| MUS | Mauritius | 2017 | 2016 |
| MWI | Malawi | 2015 | 2016 |
| NAM | Namibia | 2017 | 2016 |
| NER | Niger | 2016 | 2016 |
| NGA | Nigeria | 2017 | 2016 |
| RWA | Rwanda | 2016 | 2016 |
| SDN | Sudan | — | — |

*Source:* Arenas and Vnukova 2019.

*Note:* — = not available; ISO = International Organization for Standardization.

# REFERENCE

Arenas, Guillermo, and Yulia Vnukova. 2019. "Short-Term Revenue Implications of Tariff Liberalization under the African Continental Free Trade Area (AfCFTA)." World Bank, Washington, DC.

# Appendix I: Maximizing the Potential Benefits of the African Continental Free Trade Area

AfCFTA, once completed, will be the largest free trade area in the world in terms of membership (55 countries). Free trade agreements create significant opportunities; however, the maximization of their potential benefits is not automatic. A key issue is whether and how the AfCFTA institutions and Member States may address the weaknesses that have limited the impact of previous regional trade agreements in Africa.

First and foremost, this means effectively implementing and administering the obligations of the trade agreement. It will be essential to use momentum and political attention as the new trade opportunities become reality and intra-African trade opens on January 1, 2021. The role of consumers, investors, and traders in that process will be critical to counterbalance vested interests that may resist AfCFTA reforms.

Enabling free trade goes well beyond simply removing tariffs. It means effectively addressing on-the-ground constraints that may paralyze the daily operations of ordinary producers and traders. Doing this calls for regulatory reform and, equally important, for capacity building among the institutions that enforce these regulations.

Simultaneous action is required at both the supranational and national levels. Regional communities can provide the framework for reform, for example, by bringing together regulators to define harmonized standards or to agree on mutual recognition of the qualification of professionals. Still, the responsibility for the agreement's implementation lies ultimately and equivocally with each member country.

National integration agendas must cover services as well as goods. Services are critical, job-creating inputs into the competitive edge of almost all other activities, for example, in the role that transport plays in manufacturing. To harvest the potential fruits of AfCFTA, the implementation of the agreement must be underpinned by improved trade facilitation and connectivity. The agreement's Niamey Declaration contains important provisions about trade facilitation that will need to be implemented.[1]

For historic reasons, bilateral and regional trade in the region has been hampered by trade routes designed for exporting from the continent, rather than for facilitating intra-African trade. These obstacles include long distances, inadequate transport services, and inefficient institutional and transit regimes. In many landlocked African countries, economic centers are located hundreds of kilometers away from the closest seaport. Policy makers in all member countries—particularly in transit countries— share a critical responsibility to help to overcome geographical constraints or the lack of economies of scale due to small transportation volumes. However, the experience is that many countries retain policies that favor closed, small, and inefficient services markets, and that a renewed focus on the efficiency of transport and logistics services is long overdue.

## STEPS TO MAXIMIZE THE POTENTIAL BENEFITS OF THE AGREEMENT

To a great extent, whether or not AfCFTA becomes a milestone for development in the region will depend on the following:

- The depth and breadth of detailed commitments to remove trade barriers that are to be negotiated
- The extent to which AfCFTA commitments are effectively implemented on the ground
- The specific complementary initiatives ensuring a smooth transition to free trade and inducing greater flows of productive investment in nontraditional sectors, leading to more and better jobs.

The implementation of the obligations in the trade agreement will likely prove challenging for many Member States; the lessons from previous attempts to implement international agreements are that this should not be assumed to be automatic. AfCFTA institutions, and particularly Member States, will likely require additional support to effectively implement the agreement, as well as to identify critical bottlenecks and challenges in their economies and prioritize specific actions to ensure a smooth transition to free trade and attract increasing investment. Along with the challenges of monitoring the ongoing implementation, actions are needed to ensure fairness and a level playing field for traders.

Taking into consideration the experiences of negotiations in different parts of the developing world, three fronts are required to maximize the potential benefits of AfCFTA: treaty administration, trade-related implementation support, and transition to free trade. More details on each of these areas are presented in box I.1.

**Box I.1    Maximizing the potential benefits of a free trade agreement**

Drawing on the experience of similar negotiation exercises from other developing countries, designing a complementary agenda to maximize the potential benefits of a free trade agreement would entail the following:

*Implementation and administration of the AfCFTA agreement:* Capacity building in the form of training, direct advice, and implementation support, not only for the Ministries of Trade but also for the other often-forgotten border management agencies—especially Customs, which will now be tasked with implementing an agreement to which it may have not had any previous exposure during the negotiation phase. This capacity building is essential to enable compliance, administration and problem solving, economic monitoring, and socialization of AfCFTA.

*Trade-related institutional support for implementation:* Capacity building in agencies apart from the Ministries of Trade (in charge of trade and investment-related matters) that, in practice, affect the correct functioning of AfCFTA.

*Transition to free trade:* Sector-specific initiatives to enable domestic firms (in particular, small and medium-sized enterprises) to address the economic distortions affecting their competitiveness in a free trade environment.

## Good Practices on Treaty Administration

The relevant country authorities, and possibly the Permanent Secretariat and the regional economic communities, should be capable of undertaking the following four key functions:

- **Compliance and execution.** Undertaking the gap analysis between disciplines and commitments included in AfCFTA agreement and the domestic legislation and regulations, as well as following up on liberalization and other commitments.

- **Committee follow-up, problem solving, and dispute settlement.**[2] Leveraging the operation of the different committees and mechanisms included within the institutional framework of AfCFTA, and promoting low-cost, efficient, and transparent means of identifying and solving problems for traders and investors. It may also mean using other regional and international agreements, such as the World Trade Organization's Trade Facilitation Agreement, to address, resolve, and document concerns.

- **Information and consultation with private sector stakeholders and communication strategy for civil society.** Leveraging data obtained from economic analysis and monitoring to: (1) facilitate dialogue between the private sector and governments to agree on parallel initiatives enabling domestic business to properly transition to free trade in AfCFTA implementation; and (2) communicate simple, clear, and attractive messages to civil society in Member States about the impact of AfCFTA on the different dimensions of citizens' lives—particularly with respect to the generation of new and better jobs.

- **Economic analysis and monitoring.** Using techniques to identify and gather data necessary to measure and monitor the economic and distributional impacts of AfCFTA on key economic variables in Member States (including income, trade and investment flows, jobs, and poverty and inequality), with specific attention to the sectoral composition, gender, and geographical distribution.

## Trade-Related Implementation Support

The effective implementation of AfCFTA will entail support to several additional agencies beyond those directly responsible for administering the agreement. Several authorities usually regulate and administer procedures on various matters that will directly affect the effective operation of the norms and disciplines of the trade agreement. With the support of institutions such as the World Bank Group, countries should deploy a series of analytical tools and specialized expertise to support those agencies whose mandate directly relates to AfCFTA commitments.

Concrete activities under trade-related implementation support will include the following: benchmarking, regulatory gap analyses, economic impact assessments, economic modeling, procedural streamlining process maps, regulatory transparency assessments, and stakeholder consultations to provide specific policy and regulatory reform recommendations to fully implement the norm and spirit of the AfCFTA agreement in the following areas: (1) market access (tariff liberalization and elimination of nontariff barriers), (2) trade facilitation and border management procedures, (3) sanitary and phytosanitary measures, (4) technical barriers to trade, (5) trade remedies (safeguards, antidumping, and countervailing duties), (6) trade in services, (7) investment, and (8) competition policy.

## Transition to Free Trade

Facilitating a smooth transition to free trade entails national governments interested in addressing distortions in effective private sector performance. The activities proposed to conduct this type of function constitute the following:

- First, the identification of specific sectors that may be particularly vulnerable during the transition to free trade, and the estimation of the impact that specific AfCFTA commitments may have on domestic firms and jobs, gender, and other relevant variables.
- Second, the diagnosis of specific economic and regulatory distortions affecting the competitiveness of selected types of firms (such as small and medium-sized

| Box I.2 | Available World Bank Group support to maximize the potential benefits of AfCFTA |
|---|---|

The World Bank Group can provide support on diagnostics, solution design, and implementation follow-up in each of the follow areas:

- **Treaty Administration.** Assessment of existing organizational arrangements and resources of the AfCFTA Secretariat and within the Ministries of Trade of AfCFTA Member States regarding the four key functions required to properly administer a modern free trade agreement, capacity building for officials, and benchmarking and policy recommendations based on international good practices.
- **Treaty Implementation.** Benchmarking, regulatory gap analyses, economic impact assessments, economic modeling, procedural streamlining process maps, regulatory transparency assessments, and stakeholder consultations for each interested AfCFTA Member State; advice to fully implement the norms of AfCFTA; and the use of key performance indicators to measure the impact of reforms on the ground.
- **Transition to Free Trade.** Identification of specific sectors that may be particularly vulnerable to trade liberalization; estimation of the impacts that AfCFTA commitments may have on domestic firms and jobs, gender, and other relevant variables; planning, executing, and following up processes of information and consultation between states and the private sector in designing specific agendas for transition to free trade in the context of AfCFTA.
- Leveraging of WBG financial instruments to address specific economic and regulatory distortions affecting the competitiveness of firms, including small and medium-sized enterprises in selected sectors.

enterprises in selected sectors) and identification of successful lessons learned from relevant countries in addressing similar challenges.

- Third, good practices for the planning, execution, and follow-up processes of information and consultation between the state and the private sector to design specific agendas for the transition to free trade in the context of AfCFTA.

In conclusion, AfCFTA offers ample opportunities for development in Africa; however, its implementation will face significant challenges. Lowering and eliminating tariffs will be the easiest part. The hardest part will be enacting the nontariff and trade facilitation measures, which yield the largest potential economic gains, according to the analysis in this report. Such measures will require substantial policy reforms at the national level, indicating a long road ahead. Box I. 2 summarizes the available World Bank Group support to maximize the potential benefits of AfCFTA. Achieving its full potential depends on agreeing to ambitious liberalization and full implementation of it. Partial reforms would result in smaller effects.

## NOTES

1. According to the Niamey Declaration, all members are committed "… to leverage Trade Facilitation to promote efficient and increased trade flows across the Continent." In this context,

it urges all members to: (1) put in place statutory, regulatory, and other measures to guarantee that goods can be traded under the AfCFTA trade regime; (2) facilitate transit and other formalities for goods passing through their territories; (3) align their national development and reform strategies to AfCFTA so that the agreement delivers to the expectations of African citizens; and (4) undertake stakeholder sensitization and capacity building at the national level as part of operationalizing the AfCFTA agreement ... and to "catering for the Small to Medium cross border traders." To this end, all members will collaborate with the Regional Economic Communities "to develop a simplified trade regime that fully meets the needs of our hardworking people."

2.  For instance, the continent has varying methods and practices to ensure that only qualifying goods receive the benefits of the preferential free trade agreements. It will be important for traders and administrators alike to seek one common method for administering the rules of origin that is based on best international practices of self-assessment (rather than certification from Chambers of Commerce), administered by customs administrations, and monitored through mutual cooperation agreements among customs administrations.

# Appendix J: Short-Term Revenue Implications of Tariff Liberalization under AfCFTA

## METHODOLOGY AND DATA

The Tariff Reform Impact Simulation Tool (TRIST) simulates the short-term impacts of tariff reforms on imports and tax revenues based on a partial equilibrium model.[1] TRIST treats the demand for each product in isolation from other products and does not consider inter- and intrasectoral linkages. This tool is not designed to assess economywide impacts over the medium and long term, and it does not model new trade flows through the extensive margin.

In TRIST, the response to tariff changes is modeled in two steps. First, in the case of the African Continental Free Trade Area (AfCFTA), imports from member countries replace imports from the rest of the world as the former become relatively cheaper following the elimination of tariffs on intraregional goods. Second, the demand for imports of affected products increases because they are cheaper after tariff liberalization. The import responses in the first step are driven by exporter substitution elasticity, which is assumed constant among products, and in the second step by product-specific import demand elasticities.

TRIST uses data on imports and the amounts collected for customs duties and other taxes charged on imports (such as the value added tax, sales tax, and excise tax) at the level of the tariff line and country of origin. These data are compiled from import transactions by national customs agencies and provide exact values for tax revenues and the effective tariff rates applied to imports. These "customs data" provide the most accurate estimates of the impacts of tariff changes on imports and tax revenues. However, TRIST can also use data compiled using import values and statutory tariff and tax rates obtained from national tariff schedules ("statutory data"). Because the latter do not account for nonpreferential tariff exemptions and assume a perfect utilization rate for preferential trade agreements, significant differences in estimated impacts may arise between simulations using statutory and customs data.

A database based on import values and statutory tariffs is constructed for 48 African countries for which data are available, and it is used to simulate the impacts described shortly in the section on statutory data.[2] Data collected by national customs offices are used to obtain estimates on revenue and import impacts for 11 countries described in the section on customs data.

## DESCRIPTIVE STATISTICS

Tariffs are not the only, and usually not the most important, source of revenue from imports. Figure J.1 shows that the taxes on international trade (exports and imports) as a percentage of government revenues is less than 20 percent for about two-thirds of countries for which data are available. Figure J.2 reveals that customs duties are not the most important source of import tax revenue for most countries for which customs data are available except Nigeria and São Tomé and Príncipe: the combination of the excise and value added tax usually accounts for half to three-quarters of tax revenues collected from imports. In general, then, the taxes on international trade are not the most important source of revenue for most governments in Africa.

Collected tariff rates deviate significantly from statutory tariff rates for most countries for which data are available (table J.1). These differences could arise due to two reasons. First, the statutory rates assume that imports granted preferential treatment under trade agreements make full utilization of those preferences. However, in cases in which preference utilization is not complete, the statutory rate will be lower than the paid tariff rate reflected in the customs data. Second, the statutory data assume that imports from non–free trade agreement (FTA) origins pay most-favored-nation (MFN) tariffs, which neglects the presence of nonpreferential tariff exemptions granted under the national schemes that are widespread in Africa (such as special economic zones, investment attraction packages, and industrialization plans). In countries in which these exemptions are important, the statutory rate will be higher than the effectively paid rate calculated using customs data.

**Figure J.1**    Taxes on international trade as percentage of government revenues

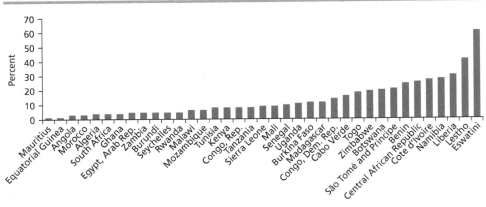

*Source:* World Bank's World Development Indicators (WDI) database (https://databank.worldbank.org /source/world-development-indicators#).

**Figure J.2**    Share of total tax revenues from imports

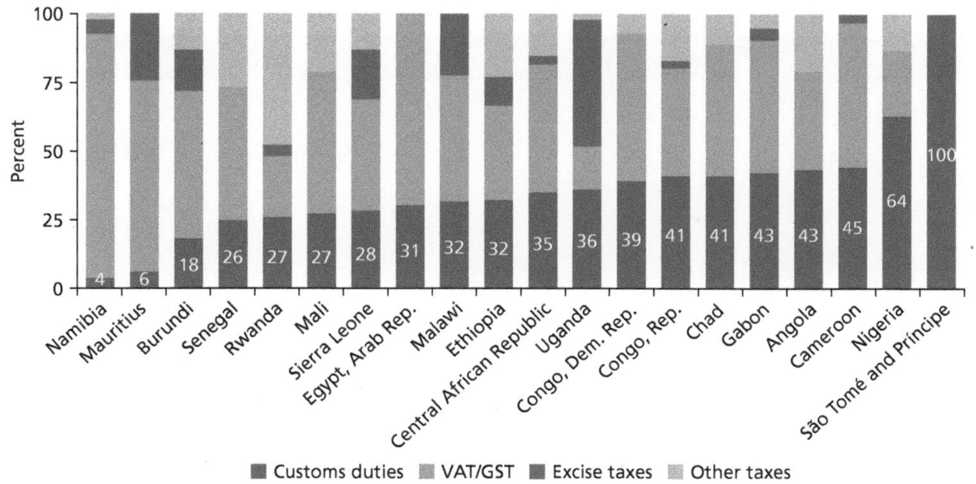

Source: Calculations based on customs data, World Bank study team.

Note: GST = general services tax; VAT = value added tax.

**Table J.1**    Statutory and collected tariff rates

|  | Statutory tariff rate | Collected tariff rate | Collected to statutory rate ratio |
|---|---|---|---|
| Chad | 15.5 | 15.5 | 1.00 |
| Cameroon | 12.9 | 10.8 | 0.84 |
| Senegal | 7.2 | 5.9 | 0.82 |
| Mauritius | 0.9 | 0.7 | 0.78 |
| Central African Republic | 14.4 | 10.1 | 0.70 |
| Angola | 8.0 | 5.5 | 0.69 |
| Gabon | 12.9 | 8.0 | 0.62 |
| Ethiopia | 10.0 | 6.1 | 0.61 |
| Congo, Dem. Rep. | 7.4 | 4.1 | 0.55 |
| Burundi | 12.3 | 6.7 | 0.54 |
| Congo, Rep. | 12.7 | 5.7 | 0.45 |
| Rwanda | 12.1 | 5.3 | 0.44 |
| São Tomé and Príncipe | 8.7 | 2.9 | 0.33 |

Source: Calculations based on customs data, World Bank study team.

Table J.2    Tariff revenue changes under AfCFTA scenario
*average annual percent change*

|  | AfCFTA liberalization | Full liberalization |
|---|---|---|
| Burundi | −1.13 | −2.01 |
| Egypt, Arab Rep. | 0.00 | −0.02 |
| Ethiopia | −0.27 | −0.40 |
| Malawi | −2.01 | −2.27 |
| Mali | −3.31 | −3.53 |
| Mauritius | −0.01 | −0.55 |
| Namibia | −0.04 | −0.09 |
| Nigeria | −0.31 | −0.47 |
| Senegal | −0.09 | −0.21 |
| Sierra Leone | −0.52 | −0.68 |
| Uganda | −0.23 | −0.30 |

*Source:* Calculations based on customs data, World Bank study team.

*Note:* AfCFTA = African Continental Free Trade Area.

## SIMULATION RESULTS USING CUSTOMS DATA

Despite fears about fiscal losses from AfCFTA, the initial short-term tax revenue losses will be small (less than 1 percent for most countries) and distributed over a decade. Average annual tariff revenue losses are estimated in table J.2 to be a 1 percent change for most countries except for Burundi (1.1 percent), Malawi (2.0 percent), and Mali (3.3 percent). However, because of the liberalization timeline, most of the revenue impact will materialize only after the fifth year when sensitive products are liberalized. The fiscal effect of AfCFTA will be small because intraregional trade and its share of tariff revenue are low in most countries.

Tariff revenue losses are estimated to be even smaller as a share of government revenue (table J.3). AfCFTA will result in annual revenue losses that do not exceed 0.06 percent of total government revenue on average during the liberalization period with the exception of Mali (0.5 percent).

## SIMULATION RESULTS USING STATUTORY DATA

Tariff revenue losses will remain below 1.5 percent for most countries, or below 0.3 percent of total tax revenues, with a few exceptions (figures J.3 and J.4). Average annual tariff revenue losses will remain below 1.5 percent for most countries except

**Table J.3**   Tax revenue changes under AfCFTA liberalization scenario

*percent*

| | Tariff revenue loss (% of tariff revenue) | Tariff revenue loss (% of total government revenue) |
|---|---|---|
| Burundi | −1.13 | −0.028 |
| Egypt, Arab Rep. | 0.00 | 0.000 |
| Ethiopia | −0.27 | −0.001 |
| Malawi | −2.01 | −0.060 |
| Mali | −3.31 | −0.493 |
| Mauritius | −0.01 | 0.000 |
| Namibia | −0.04 | 0.000 |
| Nigeria | −0.31 | −0.034 |
| Senegal | −0.09 | 0.003 |
| Sierra Leone | −0.52 | −0.045 |
| Uganda | −0.23 | −0.038 |

*Source:* Calculations based on customs data and International Monetary Fund (IMF) Article IV reports and on the IMF's Global Financial Statistics (https://data.imf.org/?sk=a0867067-d23c-4ebc-ad23-d3b015045405), using the latest year available—Burundi (2013), Ethiopia (2013), Malawi (2017), Mali (2016), Mauritius (2017), Namibia (2019), Nigeria (2018), Senegal (2019), Sierra Leone (2014), Uganda (2016)—World Bank study team.

*Note:* AfCFTA = African Continental Free Trade Area.

the Democratic Republic of Congo (3.4 percent), The Gambia (2.7 percent), the Republic of Congo (2.1 percent), and Zambia (1.6 percent). However, because of the liberalization timeline, most of the revenue impacts will materialize only after the fifth year when sensitive products are liberalized (see table J.4 for a yearly breakdown of tariff revenue impacts). However, even in countries experiencing the largest tariff revenue losses, lost revenues as a percentage of total government revenues is rarely expected to rise above a 0.3 percent annual change. These results are consistent with other partial equilibrium estimations (UNECA 2017) that show that the number of countries with high tariff revenue losses is reduced, even under full liberalization.

## COMPARISON OF RESULTS USING CUSTOMS AND STATUTORY DATA

The differences in estimated tariff revenue losses depend on whether one is using customs data or statutory data (table J.5). For some countries such as the Arab Republic of Egypt, Senegal, Sierra Leone, and Uganda, the percentage estimates using statutory data are higher than the estimates using the actual customs data, while for the

**Figure J.3**    Average annual change in tariff revenue (average annual percent change)

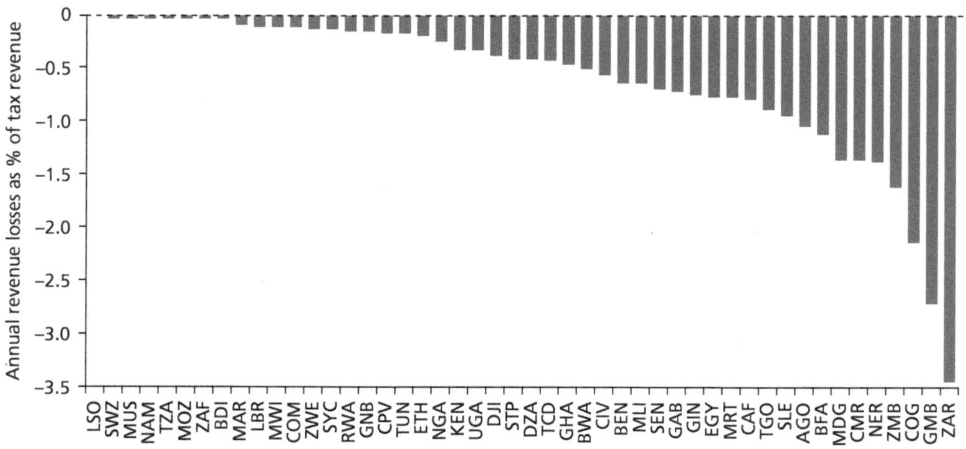

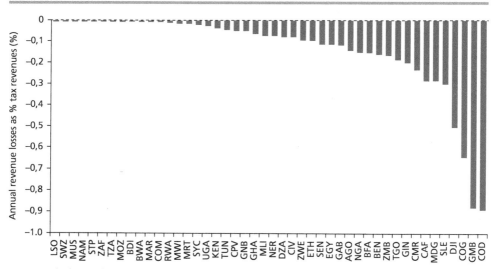

*Source:* Calculations based on statutory data, World Bank study team.

*Note:* See table J.4 for country abbreviations.

**Figure J.4**    Average annual change in tax revenue (percent of tax revenue)

*Source:* Calculations based on statutory data, World Bank study team.

*Note:* Countries for which total government revenue data were available in the International Monetary Fund's Global Financial Statistics (https://data.imf.org/?sk=a0867067-d23c-4ebc-ad23-d3b015045405). See table J.4 for country abbreviations.

Table J.4    Simulation results based on statutory data

*percent of tariff revenue*

|  | Year 1 | Year 2 | Year 3 | Year 4 | Year 5 | Year 6 | Year 7 | Year 8 | Year 9 | Year 10 |
|---|---|---|---|---|---|---|---|---|---|---|
| AGO | −0.046 | −0.046 | −0.046 | −0.046 | −0.046 | −2.00 | −2.00 | −2.00 | −2.00 | −2.00 |
| BDI | 0.000 | 0.000 | 0.000 | 0.000 | 0.000 | −0.05 | −0.05 | −0.05 | −0.05 | −0.05 |
| BEN | −0.003 | −0.003 | −0.003 | −0.003 | −0.003 | −1.23 | −1.23 | −1.23 | −1.23 | −1.23 |
| BFA | −0.014 | −0.014 | −0.014 | −0.014 | −0.014 | −2.20 | −2.20 | −2.20 | −2.20 | −2.20 |
| BWA | 0.000 | 0.000 | 0.000 | 0.000 | 0.000 | −0.99 | −0.99 | −0.99 | −0.99 | −0.99 |
| CAF | 0.000 | 0.000 | 0.000 | 0.000 | 0.000 | −1.54 | −1.54 | −1.54 | −1.54 | −1.54 |
| CIV | −0.013 | −0.013 | −0.013 | −0.013 | −0.013 | −1.09 | −1.09 | −1.09 | −1.09 | −1.09 |
| CMR | −0.006 | −0.006 | −0.006 | −0.006 | −0.006 | −2.69 | −2.69 | −2.69 | −2.69 | −2.69 |
| COG | −0.006 | −0.006 | −0.006 | −0.006 | −0.006 | −4.25 | −4.25 | −4.25 | −4.25 | −4.25 |
| COM | 0.000 | 0.000 | 0.000 | 0.000 | 0.000 | −0.22 | −0.22 | −0.22 | −0.22 | −0.22 |
| CPV | 0.000 | 0.000 | 0.000 | 0.000 | 0.000 | −0.31 | −0.31 | −0.31 | −0.31 | −0.31 |
| DJI | 0.000 | 0.000 | 0.000 | 0.000 | 0.000 | −0.73 | −0.73 | −0.73 | −0.73 | −0.73 |
| DZA | −0.007 | −0.007 | −0.007 | −0.007 | −0.007 | −0.79 | −0.79 | −0.79 | −0.79 | −0.79 |
| EGY | 0.000 | 0.000 | 0.000 | 0.000 | 0.000 | −1.51 | −1.51 | −1.51 | −1.51 | −1.51 |
| ETH | −0.002 | −0.002 | −0.002 | −0.002 | −0.002 | −0.36 | −0.36 | −0.36 | −0.36 | −0.36 |
| GAB | −0.006 | −0.006 | −0.006 | −0.006 | −0.006 | −1.38 | −1.38 | −1.38 | −1.38 | −1.38 |
| GHA | −0.036 | −0.036 | −0.036 | −0.036 | −0.036 | −0.85 | −0.85 | −0.85 | −0.85 | −0.85 |
| GIN | −0.003 | −0.003 | −0.003 | −0.003 | −0.003 | −1.48 | −1.48 | −1.48 | −1.48 | −1.48 |
| GMB | 0.000 | 0.000 | 0.000 | 0.000 | 0.000 | −5.40 | −5.40 | −5.40 | −5.40 | −5.40 |
| GNB | 0.000 | 0.000 | 0.000 | 0.000 | 0.000 | −0.30 | −0.30 | −0.30 | −0.30 | −0.30 |
| KEN | −0.009 | −0.009 | −0.009 | −0.009 | −0.009 | −0.61 | −0.61 | −0.61 | −0.61 | −0.61 |
| LBR | 0.000 | 0.000 | 0.000 | 0.000 | 0.000 | −0.21 | −0.21 | −0.21 | −0.21 | −0.21 |
| LSO | 0.000 | 0.000 | 0.000 | 0.000 | 0.000 | 0.00 | 0.00 | 0.00 | 0.00 | 0.00 |
| MAR | 0.000 | 0.000 | 0.000 | 0.000 | 0.000 | −0.16 | −0.16 | −0.16 | −0.16 | −0.16 |
| MDG | −0.027 | −0.027 | −0.027 | −0.027 | −0.027 | −2.67 | −2.67 | −2.67 | −2.67 | −2.67 |
| MLI | −0.019 | −0.019 | −0.019 | −0.019 | −0.019 | −1.22 | −1.22 | −1.22 | −1.22 | −1.22 |
| MOZ | 0.000 | 0.000 | 0.000 | 0.000 | 0.000 | −0.03 | −0.03 | −0.03 | −0.03 | −0.03 |
| MRT | −0.002 | −0.002 | −0.002 | −0.002 | −0.002 | −1.52 | −1.52 | −1.52 | −1.52 | −1.52 |
| MUS | 0.000 | 0.000 | 0.000 | 0.000 | 0.000 | 0.00 | 0.00 | 0.00 | 0.00 | 0.00 |
| MWI | 0.000 | 0.000 | 0.000 | 0.000 | 0.000 | −0.21 | −0.21 | −0.21 | −0.21 | −0.21 |
| NAM | 0.000 | 0.000 | 0.000 | 0.000 | 0.000 | −0.01 | −0.01 | −0.01 | −0.01 | −0.01 |

*continued*

**Table J.4**  Simulation results based on statutory data *(continued)*

*percent of tariff revenue*

|        | Year 1 | Year 2 | Year 3 | Year 4 | Year 5 | Year 6 | Year 7 | Year 8 | Year 9 | Year 10 |
|--------|--------|--------|--------|--------|--------|--------|--------|--------|--------|---------|
| NER    | −0.005 | −0.005 | −0.005 | −0.005 | −0.005 | −2.74  | −2.74  | −2.74  | −2.74  | −2.74   |
| NGA    | −0.010 | −0.010 | −0.010 | −0.010 | −0.010 | −0.46  | −0.46  | −0.46  | −0.46  | −0.46   |
| RWA    | −0.005 | −0.005 | −0.005 | −0.005 | −0.005 | −0.28  | −0.28  | −0.28  | −0.28  | −0.28   |
| SEN    | −0.006 | −0.006 | −0.006 | −0.006 | −0.006 | −1.36  | −1.36  | −1.36  | −1.36  | −1.36   |
| SLE    | −0.002 | −0.002 | −0.002 | −0.002 | −0.002 | −1.86  | −1.86  | −1.86  | −1.86  | −1.86   |
| STP    | −0.004 | −0.004 | −0.004 | −0.004 | −0.004 | −0.76  | −0.76  | −0.76  | −0.76  | −0.76   |
| SWZ    | 0.000  | 0.000  | 0.000  | 0.000  | 0.000  | 0.00   | 0.00   | 0.00   | 0.00   | 0.00    |
| SYC    | 0.000  | 0.000  | 0.000  | 0.000  | 0.000  | −0.26  | −0.26  | −0.26  | −0.26  | −0.26   |
| TCD    | 0.000  | 0.000  | 0.000  | 0.000  | 0.000  | −0.82  | −0.82  | −0.82  | −0.82  | −0.82   |
| TGO    | −0.001 | −0.001 | −0.001 | −0.001 | −0.001 | −1.76  | −1.76  | −1.76  | −1.76  | −1.76   |
| TUN    | 0.000  | 0.000  | 0.000  | 0.000  | 0.000  | −0.33  | −0.33  | −0.33  | −0.33  | −0.33   |
| TZA    | 0.000  | 0.000  | 0.000  | 0.000  | 0.000  | −0.02  | −0.02  | −0.02  | −0.02  | −0.02   |
| UGA    | −0.012 | −0.012 | −0.012 | −0.012 | −0.012 | −0.63  | −0.63  | −0.63  | −0.63  | −0.63   |
| ZAF    | 0.000  | 0.000  | 0.000  | 0.000  | 0.000  | −0.05  | −0.05  | −0.05  | −0.05  | −0.05   |
| ZAR    | −0.294 | −0.294 | −0.294 | −0.294 | −0.294 | −6.58  | −6.58  | −6.58  | −6.58  | −6.58   |
| ZMB    | 0.000  | 0.000  | 0.000  | 0.000  | 0.000  | −3.20  | −3.20  | −3.20  | −3.20  | −3.20   |
| ZWE    | 0.000  | 0.000  | 0.000  | 0.000  | 0.000  | −0.24  | −0.24  | −0.24  | −0.24  | −0.24   |

*Note:* AGO = Angola; BDI = Burundi; BEN = Benin; BFA = Burkina Faso; BWA = Botswana; CAF = Central African Republic; CIV = Côte d'Ivoire; CMR = Cameroon; COG = Republic of Congo; COM = Comoros; CPV = Cabo Verde; DJI = Djibouti; DZA = Algeria; EGY = Arab Republic of Egypt; ETH = Ethiopia; GAB = Gabon; GHA = Ghana; GIN = Guinea; GMB = The Gambia; GNB = Guinea-Bissau; KEN = Kenya; LBR = Liberia; LSO = Lesotho; MAR = Morocco; MDG = Madagascar; MLI = Mali; MOZ = Mozambique; MRT = Mauritania; MUS = Mauritius; MWI = Malawi; NAM = Namibia; NER = Niger; NGA = Nigeria; RWA = Rwanda; SEN = Senegal; SLE = Sierra Leone; STP = São Tomé and Príncipe; SWZ = Eswatini; SYC = Seychelles; TCD = Chad; TGO = Togo; TUN = Tunisia; TZA = Tanzania; UGA = Uganda; ZAF = South Africa; ZAR = Democratic Republic of Congo; ZMB = Zambia; ZWE = Zimbabwe.

remaining countries the customs data estimates are lower. For example, in Egypt, the statutory data estimates of tariff revenues are significantly higher (more negative) when compared with the actual customs data (−0.8 percent versus −0.001 percent). Likewise, Senegal's tariff revenue losses using statutory data are seven times higher than the estimates using customs data (−0.7 percent versus −0.1 percent). Among the remaining countries in table J.5, the revenue losses estimated with customs data are higher than those estimated with statutory data, ranging from 40 times higher (Burundi) to only 1.3 times higher (Nigeria). Despite the differences in results, the average tariff revenue impact of AfCFTA is small no matter which data are used, with most countries in

**Table J.5**  Import and tariff revenue impacts estimated using customs data and statutory data

*percent*

| | Tariff revenues | |
|---|---|---|
| | Customs data | Statutory data |
| Burundi | −1.10 | −0.03 |
| Egypt, Arab Rep. | −0.001 | −0.76 |
| Ethiopia | −0.30 | −0.18 |
| Malawi | −2.00 | −0.11 |
| Mali | −3.30 | −0.62 |
| Mauritius | −0.01 | 0.00 |
| Namibia | −0.04 | −0.01 |
| Nigeria | −0.30 | −0.24 |
| Senegal | −0.10 | −0.68 |
| Sierra Leone | −0.50 | −0.93 |
| Uganda | −0.20 | −0.32 |

*Source:* Calculations based on customs and statutory data, World Bank study team.

table J.5 experiencing losses of less than 1 percent according to customs data and all countries experiencing losses of less than 1 percent according to statutory data.

Three reasons may explain the differences in the results obtained using customs and statutory data: (1) different import values; (2) import origin composition; and (3) applied tariff rates. Specifically, first, the two data sets may have different total import values. Estimated impacts would then be overestimated in the data set with the largest values. Second, the two data sets may have different shares of imports originating from AfCFTA countries. If one data set significantly overestimates (underestimates) the percentage of imports from AfCFTA countries, then, all else being equal, the impact on imports of removing tariffs on AfCFTA countries will be larger (smaller). Third, the two data sets may have different tariff rates applied to AfCFTA countries. In this case, eliminating tariffs on AfCFTA countries using the data set with the larger (smaller) applied tariffs would result in larger (smaller) impacts on imports, assuming that elasticities remain the same.

The difference in import values is significant for Ethiopia, Mali, and Malawi. Differences between statutory and customs total import values are generally less than 10 percentage points for most countries in the sample (figure J.5). However, even though differences in Ethiopia are large, the value recorded in the customs database matches the official import value reported by the statistical agency, whereas the value from COMTRADE exceeds it by almost 50 percent.

**Figure J.5**   Ratio of statutory to customs import values

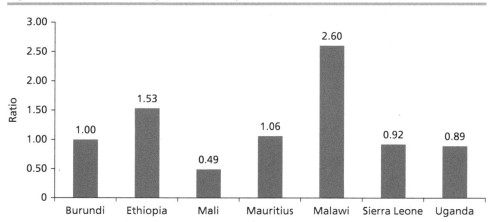

*Source:* Calculations based on customs and statutory data, World Bank study team.

**Figure J.6**   Imports from AfCFTA countries, statutory and customs

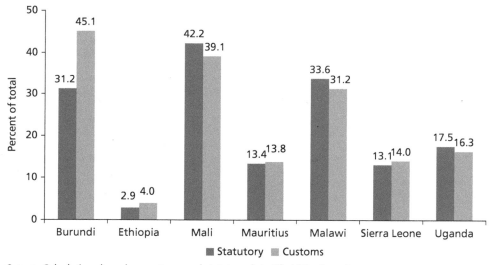

*Source:* Calculations based on customs and statutory data, World Bank study team.

*Note:* AfCFTA = African Continental Free Trade Area.

Differences in the percentage of imports originating from AfCFTA are small except for Burundi. Figure J.6 shows the share of total imports of AfCFTA countries, calculated using customs and statutory data. The differences are smaller than 3 percentage points for all countries except Burundi, whose AfCFTA share of imports is 14 percentage points higher in the customs database (45 percent) than in the statutory database (31 percent).

**Figure J.7**   Effective tariff rates for AfCFTA countries (weighted average)

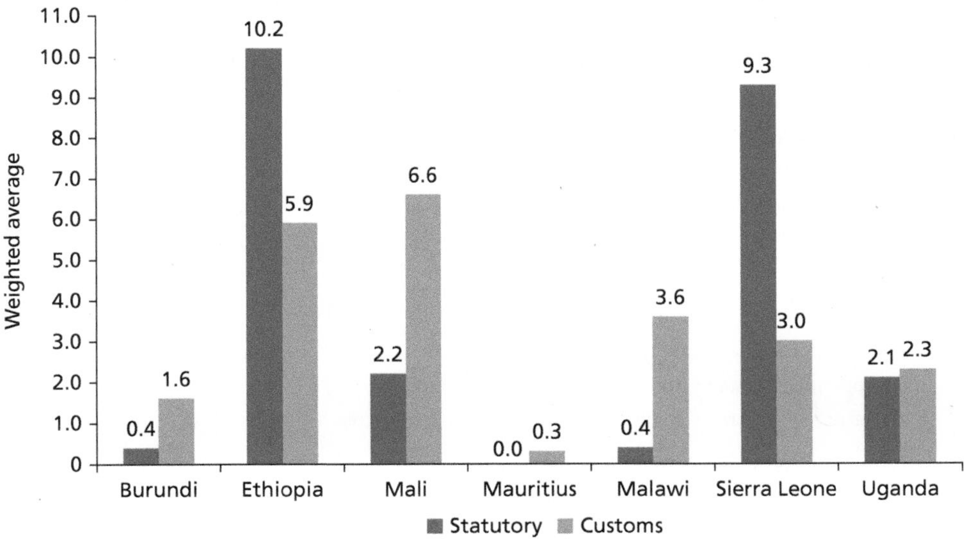

*Source:* Calculations based on customs and statutory data, World Bank study team.
*Note:* AfCFTA = African Continental Free Trade Area.

Differences in tariff rates applied to AfCFTA imports are significant in most countries except Uganda and Mauritius (figure J.7). These differences may arise from two reasons. First, the statutory data assume, by construction, that imports granted preferential treatment under current trade agreements fully utilize those preferences. In cases in which the preference utilization is not 100 percent, the statutory rate will be higher than the effectively paid tariff rate, which is reflected in the customs data. Second, the statutory data assume that imports not affected by preferential rates pay MFN tariffs, which neglects the presence of nonpreferential tariff exemptions granted under the national schemes that are widespread in Africa (such as special economic zones, investment attraction packages, and industrialization plans). In countries in which these exemptions are important, the statutory rate will be higher than the effectively paid rate in the customs data.

## CONCLUSIONS

The results of the simulations reveal that the short-term impacts of AfCFTA on imports and tax revenues are small for most countries. Increases in imports are expected to remain below 0.5 percent. Tariff revenue losses will remain below 1 percent for roughly two-thirds of countries. Even in countries experiencing the largest tariff revenue losses, the decline in terms of total government revenues is rarely expected to rise above 0.3 percent. These results are consistent with other studies that show that, even under full liberalization, the number of countries that will experience significant tariff revenue losses is small and that exclusion lists have the potential to significantly reduce such losses (ADB 2019; UNECA 2017).

The results also show that there could be significant differences in estimates using customs and statutory data, although both sets of data point to lower impacts overall. Collected tariff rates deviate significantly from statutory tariff rates for most countries for which data are available, and it is not possible to predict the direction or magnitude of the difference with the available data. An effort should be made to collect customs data for most African countries to corroborate the results of the statutory simulations.

## NOTES

1. This appendix is based on Arenas and Vnukova (2019).
2. No statutory data are available for Equatorial Guinea, Eritrea, Libya, Somalia, South Sudan, and Sudan.

## REFERENCES

ADB (African Development Bank). 2019. *African Economic Outlook 2019.* Abidjan, Côte d'Ivoire: ADB.

Arenas, Guillermo, and Yulia Vnukova. 2019. "Short-Term Revenue Implications of Tariff Liberalization under the African Continental Free Trade Area (AfCFTA)." World Bank, Washington, DC.

UNECA (United Nations Economic Commission of Africa). 2017. "Assessing Regional Integration in Africa VIII: Bringing the Continental Free Trade Area About." Addis Ababa, Ethiopia.